More of and the Best of

Me
&
Snap

True Gut-Busting Tales
You Won't Be Able to Put It Down

by John Bruner

Copyright © 2017 by John Bruner.

Library of Congress Control Number: 2017901439
ISBN: Hardcover 978-1-5245-7973-9
Softcover 978-1-5245-7972-2
eBook 978-1-5245-7971-5

All rights reserved. No part of this book may be reproduced or transmitted in any form or by any means, electronic or mechanical, including photocopying, recording, or by any information storage and retrieval system, without permission in writing from the copyright owner.

Any people depicted in stock imagery provided by Thinkstock are models, and such images are being used for illustrative purposes only. Certain stock imagery © Thinkstock.

Print information available on the last page.

Rev. date: 01/28/2017

To order additional copies of this book, contact:
Xlibris
1-888-795-4274
www.Xlibris.com
Orders@Xlibris.com
755895

TABLE OF CONTENTS

FOREWORD ix
CHAPTER 1   SNAP 1
CHAPTER 2   Greenriver 5
CHAPTER 3   Stuck in the Sewer 11
CHAPTER 4   Polio Shots 19
CHAPTER 5   Books in the Britches 24
CHAPTER 6   BONK! 29
CHAPTER 7   Forts in the Jungle 33
CHAPTER 8   Coonskin Caps 39
CHAPTER 9   Killed in the Fort 43
CHAPTER 10   Where's Mom Going? 49
CHAPTER 11   Midnight Witch 53
CHAPTER 12   Trouble in Kindergarten 56
CHAPTER 13   More Trouble in Kindergarten 62
CHAPTER 14   BUSTED! 64
CHAPTER 15   Friday Night Fights 68
CHAPTER 16   Monsters & Sissies 72
CHAPTER 17   Squirt Guns 75
CHAPTER 18   Pigeon Pie & Pigeon Poop 78

CHAPTER 19	Yellow Snow	83
CHAPTER 20	Dumb & Dumb "Or"	90
CHAPTER 21	Don't Kill Fritz	96
CHAPTER 22	Three Block Fist Fight	101
CHAPTER 23	Ghost in the Attic	107
CHAPTER 24	Peashooters	112
CHAPTER 25	Killed a Cow	117
CHAPTER 26	Pooped My Pants	122
CHAPTER 27	Elevator	126
CHAPTER 28	Contraptions	131
CHAPTER 29	Snap's Been Kidnapped	135
CHAPTER 30	Battleship TITANIC	139
CHAPTER 31	Golfing Black Birds	144
CHAPTER 32	Got in Trouble	148
CHAPTER 33	Snakes in School	154
CHAPTER 34	Rumble	158
CHAPTER 35	Cornfields & Graveyards	161
CHAPTER 36	Long-Shots	168
CHAPTER 37	WHACK!	170
CHAPTER 38	Kissin' in the Chicken Coop	174
CHAPTER 39	Snap's on Fire	177
CHAPTER 40	BEER	180

More of and the Best of

Me
&
Snap

Thanks for checking out
More of and the Best of ME & SNAP.

We hope it brings you love and laughter
and sweet memories.

You can also check out our website at:
www.gutbustingtales.com

FOREWORD

The book you are holding in your hands is a stroke of genius.

My dear friend John Bruner, author of *'Me and Snap'* and *'Bonk,'* has borrowed a concept from the record industry. Musicians from Frank Sinatra to Johnny Cash to The Rolling Stones to Justin Bieber, and every talented artist in between, have learned that fans love hearing their very best songs over and over on one album.

That is exactly what John has done by combining the stories you are about to read, or reread, in this wonderful book. Thanks to hundreds of unsolicited positive comments he's received from attendees at his many readings, emails, phone calls, letters, and folks stopping him on the street, John knows which tales garnered the most smiles or tears.

And if all that is not good enough, here is something even better! Included along with the wonderful *old* stories, the talented author has inserted some brand *new* ones for your reading pleasure.

When he first expressed the idea of combining these wonderful vignettes into one **'Best of'** book to me, I immediately *thought* that it was a wonderful and creative idea. Now that I've actually seen his choices while rereading the laugh-out-loud stories ... and enjoying the brand new ones, I *know* that it was a wonderful and creative idea!

The author has a God-given gift of storytelling. He knows exactly how to pull at your heartstrings or tickle your funny bone ... sometimes in the same paragraph. Best of all, when he writes about a prank that he and his brother Snap pulled, such as golfing dead blackbirds into a neighbor's yard with a 9-iron, you will be reminded of some crazy episode from your own youth.

A word of warning: you need to know here and now that John's stories are like potato chips. Once you start, there's no way to stop at one. If you are an owner of the original books, welcome back.

If you're a first-timer, you are in for a great treat.

Thanks, John, for bringing back to life tales of two little boys from Middle America USA in the 1950s. I am thrilled that both new and original readers are about to share in the antics of *'Me and Snap.'*

It has been said that love is even better "the second time around." And I think that the same will be said about this book.

Bill Sheridan, Author and Writing Coach
www.sheridanwrites.com
February 2013

Chapter 1

SNAP

"Lights Out"

Dateline: Summer, 1957 – Ages 13 & 12

I was born May 22, 1944 and christened John William Bruner. I received John from my grandfather, John Bruner. William was my grandfather Cavanaugh's first name and I have been honored to carry their good names through another generation.

Many people, for various reasons, get tagged with a nickname that sticks for a lifetime. Well, when I was a kid my nickname was "John." When I was a school kid my nickname was "John." When I married my high school sweetheart my nickname was "John." And now getting up in years, my friends and family still call me by my nickname, "John." At first it was hard for me to accept the nickname John, but I've learned to deal with it and when people ask me how I happen to get the nickname "John" I simply tell them, "My brother Snap stuck me with it."

How did he choose the nickname John, they ask? I tell them, "I'm not sure, but he's been calling me that since we were little kids––and it has stuck ever since. He was just a clever little fella!"

Snap was born November 5, 1945, christened Robert Brian Bruner. Robert was our father's name. Brian was someone else's name and Bruner was grandpa's last name. So, where did "Snap" come from?

Well, back in Carroll, Iowa in the '50s, Snap was a young man's man––or something like that. The truth is, I think he discovered hormones before hormones became popular. Anyway, he came by his nickname "Snap" very honestly and with no regrets. I know this to be true because I was there the night he became "Snap." I witnessed it, and as sure as he was the one that stuck me with the nickname "John," I was the one who stuck him with the nickname "Snap."

Sweet Revenge. I LOVE IT.

Oh, the story? Yes, of course. It's important that all the facts be known.

It was a hot summer night in 1957. We were at home in the Boys' Room just kinda pounding on each other for lack of anything better to do when the phone rang. It was for Snap. He asked who it was and Mom said, "Mike."

At that time in our lives no one's voices had changed yet, so the girls sounded like boys and the boys sounded like girls. Nobody could tell the difference and nobody really cared. But this night, Mike was not Mike. Mike was Micki. She just became Mike when Mom answered the phone.

Micki had called to tell Snap that she was home babysitting her younger brothers and was about to put them to bed and was just wondering if he might want to come over and watch television with her. His answer was, "I'll be right over."

Now Micki was the cutest little 12-year-old girl on the planet. What she ever saw in Snap is still one of the world's great mysteries. Anyway, Snap told me where he was going and I asked him, "What for?"

He said, "None of your business."

Big mistake. Big, big mistake.

So when he left the house I called my buddy Cy Farner who just lived across the street. I told him what was going on, so we joined up in his back yard and headed for Micki's house. When we got there, through window-peeking surveillance, we saw them sitting next to each other on the couch. We were really surprised because at that time none of us had held a girl's hand or even thought about kissing one of them.

But now, tonight, all that was going to change. That skinny little 12-year-old brother of mine was going to change the world as we knew it.

Cy and I were not ready for this. We were still kids. Girls were ugly, dumb, loud, stupid, and always trying to be teacher's pet. Really, what were they good for? I guess Snap knew and we didn't. Hate it when that happens.

Well, as Snap was sliding closer and closer to Micki, Cy and I were pushing and shoving each other for a better window position. And darned if we didn't get the church giggles. Oh those church giggles, they got us in more trouble than just in church. But that's another story. Anyway, back to Snap. He heard the laughter, whispered something to Micki, got off the couch, checked the windows and before we knew it ...

ALL THE LIGHTS WENT ... SNAP!

Chapter 2

GREENRIVER

"It was a good day!"

Dateline: 1952

We weren't very big, but we were in big trouble. I can't remember exactly what it was that me and Snap did, but it had something to do with stuff being broken.

Anyway, Mom said, "Boys, out of the house and go to your father's office."

"Oh, no! Not the office!"

We begged her! We pleaded with her! We apologized, but to no avail. She just looked at us and ordered, "Get moving, *NOW!*"

Dad's office was downtown, ten blocks away. As we were making that long, scary journey, we visited about what punishment was awaiting us. We would probably get a spanking and that was okay, because at least it would be over with quickly.

We might be sent to the Boys' Room with no supper that evening. That was okay, too, because we had some candy stashed in secret places in the Boys' Room.

Boys' Town? We didn't want to go there. It's too far from home. And, if we decided to leave there we might get lost on our way home.

What if Dad took our weekly allowance away from us? That would be terrible. Every Saturday morning he would give us each 25 cents and we'd head downtown and go to the cowboy movie, either at the State Theater or the Carroll Theater. It cost a dime to get in, a nickel for a generous sack of popcorn, and a dime for a cup of pop that came out of a nifty, pushbutton machine. It didn't get any better than that!

When the movie was over, we'd always stop at Pokey's Malt Shop and buy one of the best caramel apples in the whole world. The owners of Pokey's, Mr. and Mrs. Pollastrini, were the nicest people in the world. They were always happy to see us and even let us pick out the exact caramel apple we wanted. The cost? 10 cents! Where did we get the extra dime? We each had piggy banks and saved for these important occasions.

As we got closer to Dad's place, we fell silent. His office was above Leman's Drug Store. We walked up those old, dark wooden stairs flushed with guilt, opened the door, and stepped in. We were greeted with a smile by his nice secretary. She told us to sit down and Dad would see us in a little while.

We sat down and didn't make a peep. The wait of a "little while" seemed like hours. Maybe it *was* hours. Our little brains weren't computing much at that stressful time.

Finally, Dad opened his office door and said, "Okay boys, come in."

With heads bowed, we marched in and sat down.

"What are you boys doing here?"

"Mom got mad and sent us to see you."

"What did you do to make her so mad?"

"We were wrestling and accidently broke some stuff."

"Didn't your mother tell you to go outside and wrestle?"

"Yes."

"And, why didn't you?"

"We were on our way outside and then started wrestling again and then things just started breaking."

Dad didn't say anything for a little bit. We were too scared to look at him, but me and Snap think maybe we said something that made him smile. Don't know for sure.

"Boys, it's time this behavior stops, and stops NOW! So, what am I going to do with you? What punishment do you deserve?"

"Spanking?"

"Maybe?"

"Go to bed with no supper?"

"Maybe?"

"Go to Boys' Town for a couple of days?"

That seemed to make Dad feel good, because we looked up and he was smiling.

"No, you are not going to Boys' Town."

Whew, that was close!

"Are you going to take our allowance away?"

"No, I'm not taking your allowance away. I am not going to spank you, and I'm not going to send you to bed without supper."

"You're not?"

"No. I'm going to have you do something that will make your mom feel good. I want you to tell your mom three things, and I want you to MEAN IT! Okay?"

"Okay."

"Before supper tonight you tell your mother that: 1) You are sorry for being bad; 2) She is a good mom and you love her; and 3) You will never be bad again. Can you do that?"

"Yes."

"Okay, let's go to Vince & Jim's for a greenriver and some donuts."

Vince & Jim's was the malt shop on the other end of the block. They had a machine that made the world's best donuts. And they were really nice people. They were always happy. I remember Vince and his wife Dorothy. Wow, they were cool!

Anyway, me and Snap were shocked. After all the bad things we did, Dad took us to Vince & Jim's for donuts and greenrivers. We knew we weren't very smart, but we sure couldn't figure this one out.

Dad then sent us home and said he'd be there in a little while. As we were walking home, we reviewed what we had to tell Mom. When we got to that "never" part, we tried to figure out how long "never" was. We weren't sure, but we agreed it was about 100 weeks. When Dad got home, he called us into the living room. Mom was standing there.

Dad turned to Mom and said, "Lorraine, the boys have something to tell you."

"Okay boys, what is it?"

"Mom, we are sorry that we were bad, and you are the best mom ever, and we love you, and we will never be bad again."

"Boys, never is a long time. Do you know how long NEVER is?"

"Yes."

"How long is NEVER?"

"It's a hundred weeks."

That made her happy that we knew how long NEVER was, because she turned to Dad and smiled really big and he smiled back.

Then Mom asked us, "If never is a hundred weeks, how many days is that?"

Well, we weren't prepared for that one, so we just took a wild guess at it.

"A hundred weeks is about 300 days."

Talk about a lucky guess! That really made her and Dad happy because they both starting laughing really loud. That was a good sign.

Mom reached out and gave us both a hug and told us to go wash our hands and get ready for supper.

Wow! No spanking; no Boys' Town! We got supper and we got our allowance! And to top it off, we each had a greenriver and three of Vince & Jim's donuts ... WOW ...

IT WAS A GOOD DAY!

Chapter 3

STUCK IN THE SEWER

"RATS"

Dateline: Late Summer 1952 – Ages 8 & 7

It was a hot, early September day and we had just had a great thunderstorm that dropped a whole bunch of rain on Carroll. Whenever that happened, our street flooded and we were out there as soon as the lightning stopped. We would get on our bikes and take about a block run at the flood and see how far we could go before being pulverized by the sheer depth of the water.

On this particular day, we became curious about where the water was disappearing to. As it got lower and lower, we saw the big mouth of the storm sewer swallowing our fun-time flood waters. When the water was all gone, we moved in for a closer look. We got down on our knees, looked down into the sewer, and got very interested in it. It had great "Fort" potential.

The next day after school, we made a quick apple raid and headed for the sewer.

"Apple raid?"

Well, almost every house in Carroll had some kind of fruit tree, so when things ripened, we would grab our salt-shakers (we all had our own shakers) and go shopping for the juiciest fruit in the neighborhood. Most of the neighbors didn't care if we picked an apple or two, but on a couple of occasions, when we started throwing apples at each other and accidentally hit their house, they would holler at us, "Get the hell out of here you little sh_ _s."

Lots of the older people in the neighborhood used to call us that. Anyway, on this day, Snap, Cy Farner and I decided to see if we were skinny enough to squeeze down into that sewer. It had a big, horizontal mouth on it and––guess what?––we slipped right down like sliced bread into a toaster! It was nice down there––kinda dark––but what a great fort! No one could see or find us down there if we were hiding. Perfect. It was our "foxhole fort" and the war games could begin.

We went down there quite a bit and always took our fruit and BB guns with us because, in a real war, the army guys always had their guns and food in the foxholes. We would tell secrets down there, shoot at some of the rats that would occasionally visit, and shoot at birds and squirrels on the other side of the street.

One day as we were walking to our fox hole, a lady from across the street came over and told us someone had shot out one of her windows with what appeared to be a BB gun. She rather tersely asked, "Did you boys do it?"

We told her that we don't shoot our BB guns around houses.

She said, "Well, you have your BB guns with you now and there are nothing but houses all around. So, where are you going to shoot those guns today?"

Snap came up with the perfect answer. "See that sewer? There are rats down there and we are going down there to shoot them."

The nice neighbor lady didn't say any more. She just gave us another one of those funny looks, shook her head, and walked away. That was good, because most of the grownups that got mad at us would say, "We're calling your mom and dad!"

I don't know; we didn't think we were bad kids, but it sure seemed like a lot of older people thought we were!

One late afternoon, when Snap and I were down in our fox hole, one of the neighbor girls, Suzie O'Brien, peeked in and asked what we were doing. We told her, "Playing war."

She asked if she could come down and we said, "Okay, but there's rats down here."

She didn't care. Back in those days, most of the girls that we knew weren't afraid of rats and mice and snakes. Now, Suzie was about our age, but a little thicker than we were. She pushed herself, feet first, down the mouth of the sewer. For a moment she appeared stuck, so we grabbed her ankles, gave a tug and——**plop!**——down she came. She looked around for a little bit and said, "I don't like it down here, I'm getting out."

As it turned out, it was a lot easier said than done. Suzie started crawling out, but got stuck. She was half out and half in. She was stuck tight and pleaded with us, "Please help me! Please!"

Snap crawled out and grabbed her arms; I stayed down and grabbed her feet. Snap pulled; I pushed; Suzie **CRIED**! No luck; still stuck——we tried again. Snap pulled; I pushed; Suzie **SCREAMED**! No luck; still stuck——Snap and I traded places. I pulled; Snap pushed; Suzie about **PASSED OUT**!! No luck; still stuck.

What were we going to do? Suzie was, "Stuck in the Sewer!"

We decided I should run to Suzie's house to get help. She only lived half a block away. Just as I was about to leave, Mom was standing on the front porch hollering, "Boys, come home; it's supper time!"

I hollered back, "We'll be there in a little bit!"

I knocked on the door of Suzie's house. Her mom came to the door and I told her, "Mrs. O'Brien, we need your help. Suzie is stuck in the sewer."

She exclaimed, "Oh, my God!" Then she ran right beside me all the way to the sewer. When Suzie saw her mom, she

really started crying! Mrs. O'Brien got down on her knees, grabbed Suzie's wrists, and told her she was going to pull her out.

Snap was still down in the sewer and said, "We tried that and it doesn't work."

Mrs. O'Brien looked down into the sewer at Snap and said, *"Shuuuut up!"*

For some reason, Mrs. O'Brien didn't particularly like us that day, but it was okay because back then most adults didn't like kids very much. We understood and it was okay, because we knew some day we would be adults and we probably wouldn't like little kids either. Anyway, Mrs. O'Brien gave a big pull, and ... **POP!**

Out she came.

Suzie's stomach was scratched up a little bit but, not bad. Mrs. O'Brien looked at us and said, "Do your folks know you two go down there?"

"No."

"Well, you tell them tonight, or I will. Do you understand?"

"Yes, Mrs. O'Brien."

We ran home, sat down at the supper table, and really didn't want to talk. We were hungry and kept our faces to our plates. Then, Mom asked the dreaded question. When we were being interrogated, we took turns answering every other question and, from my recollection, this is pretty much what was said.

"Where were you boys when I called you for supper?"

"We were in our fox hole."

"In your fox hole?"

"Yup."

"Where is your fox hole?"

"In the sewer in front of Moen's house."

"Oh, Good Lord! You boys don't go down in the sewer, do you?"

"Yup."

"Bob (our dad), are you listening to this?"

For some reason, Dad wasn't making eye contact with Mom, but he nodded his head yes.

"What in the world do you boys do down in that stinky old sewer?"

"Tell stories. Eat apples. Shoot rats. Play war."

"You tell stories, eat apples, shoot rats, and play war?"

"Yup."

"What kind of stories do you tell?"

"Secret ones."

"Okay. And the apples––where do you get them?"

"The neighbors' trees."

"Do you ask the neighbors if you can have them?"

"Sometimes."

Mom is looking a little stressed by now and Dad isn't looking. "You don't really shoot rats down there, do you?"

"Yup––big, fat ones."

"Do you shoot them dead?"

"No, they are too fat, but once in a while we whack them with our guns and kinda knock them silly, then we kick them and they don't bother us for a while."

"Oh, my God, there really are rats down there!"

"Yup."

"So, if you are fighting the rats down there, do you still have time to play war?"

"Yup."

"Who do you fight when you play war?"

"We fight Germans."

"Does your army have a name?"

"Yup. The Germans had a guy by the name of the Desert Fox. We really liked that name."

"So, you guys are also the Desert Fox?"

"No, the Desert Fox fought his battles in the desert and we fight our battles in the sewer, so we're the **Sewer Rats**."

"Good Lord! Okay, let me get this straight. The German guy fights in the desert, so he is the Desert Fox; and you two fight in the sewer, so you are the **Sewer Rats**?

"Yup."

About that time, Dad started coughing and when we looked at him, he had both hands over his mouth. We sure hoped he wasn't choking! He must have taken too big of a bite, because we couldn't figure out why else he would be choking.

Mom leaned forward on the table and looked right at Dad and said, "Oh, Bob, this isn't funny ...

"OUR BOYS ARE SEWER RATS!"

Chapter 4

POLIO SHOTS

Dateline: Summer, 1952 – Ages 7 & 8

Polio had struck our planet and it was scary. Mom talked about it every day and sometimes she wouldn't let us hop on our bikes and go to the swimming pool. On those days, without mom knowing, we would just hike through the Jungle and go to our other swimming hole, the Creek. We knew the Polio Bugs couldn't get us out there.

One morning, mom announced to us that a Polio vaccine was now available and we were all going to the Carroll Clinic to get a shot. We feared needles, because back then, they had to be at least two or three inches long.

"Mom, we don't want to go."

"Why?"

"It will hurt too much!"

"Oh, you tough little guys are afraid of a little tiny shot in the rear?"

"The rear? We thought it was in the arm!"

"It won't hurt. Now, let's go."

So, off we went for our Polio shots––Judy, John and Brian (Snap). When we arrived at the Carroll Clinic, they were waiting for us. They took Judy first and Mom went with her. It took about ten minutes, then she came back to the waiting area where me and Snap were. I asked her,

"Did it hurt?"

"No, but I'm tougher than you two sissies."

Judy was 12 and I have to admit, she was pretty tough for a girl. She could slug, slap, bite and scratch with the best of them. She could pound me and Snap one-on-one, but when she tried it when we were together, we'd pound her ... and she deserved it every time!

Anyway, the nurse came out and said,

"Okay John, your turn."

As I stood up to go, Snap stood up and said,

"I'm going with John."

"If that's the way you want to do it, that's okay with me. Let's go."

We went into this room that had a flat, hard bed in it and it was kinda dark. Mom was in there and said, "Snap, what are you doing here? They only do this one at a time."

"The nurse said it was okay."

Mom looked a little uncomfortable, but didn't say anything more. The doctor told me to drop my drawers (take my pants off) and lay on my stomach on that flat, hard bed. I did, and then he said,

"Now, just relax. This will just feel like a little pinch."

Well, I couldn't relax. I could just see that long needle going all the way through my rear and out my belly. I tightened up every muscle in my body and held my breath. SNAP WAS WATCHING. The doctor stuck the needle in my left bun. It hurt! I held my face in my hands, but I didn't scream and I didn't cry. Then the bad news. The doctor said I was too tight, so he would have to give me another shot in the right bun. SNAP WAS LISTENING.

The second needle crashed into my right bun. SNAP WAS WATCHING. I grunted in pain, but didn't cry. A couple of big old alligator tears rolled off my cheeks, but I didn't cry. It was over. Mom told me to go out in the waiting room with Judy. I rolled off the table, got dressed and joined Judy. But, before I left, I glanced at Snap and I could tell by the look in his eyes that all hell was about to break loose, and it did. I had just sat down by Judy and it started. Snap was screaming.

"NO! NO! NOOOOOOOO!"

The next thing we knew, Snap came running down the hall and disappeared into some other room. Mom and the doctor and three or four other nurses were hot on his trail. They caught him and, man, oh man, did he make a racket! Snap was always a fighter, so I just knew he wasn't done yet, and I was right. He broke free and sprinted down the hall. The whole place was up for grabs. Round and round and round they went. Then more adults started chasing him. What a circus! This was way too funny, but I think me and Judy were the only ones laughing.

They caught him again. As they passed by me and Judy, they were holding him straight out like a battering ram. He was mouthy and screaming and trying to get loose, but they had him this time. They disappeared into the "shot room" and closed the door. He was bellowing like a wounded bull, then all of a sudden it was quiet. I looked at Judy and said,

"I think they just killed Snap."

"No, they didn't! Don't be stupid. They just gave him the shot. It's over."

About that time, Mom and Snap came into the waiting room. Mom looked really tired. I figured she didn't sleep good the night before. That's how stupid I was. Anyway, Snap looked worn out and scraggly. His belt wasn't buckled right. His shirt was only half tucked in and his eyes were really, really red.

Mom said, "LET'S GO!

As we headed for the door, I could see something special in Snap's red eyes. He still had the tiger in him. He was still a winner. Even though it took six or seven adults to overpower him, they couldn't break his spirit.

There is something about brothers––we sense things about each other. Snap knew that I knew that he was okay and that he came out a winner. You know how I knew he knew? When we got in the car, I looked right at him and he looked right at me and ...

HE SMILED!

Chapter 5

BOOKS IN THE BRITCHES

"Sorry, We Forgot"

Dateline: 1952 – Ages 8 & 7

"Boys, up to your room; I'll be up there shortly."

We were in trouble again, and it was our own fault. Mom asked us to stop wrestling in the living room and to "take it outside," but we kept rumbling around until we broke her favorite lamp. It was 5:30 p.m. and Dad was home. Mom was both sad and mad. And Dad wasn't just mad, he was *really, really* mad!

We ran upstairs to our room and prepared for a spanking. Snap came up with a great idea––books in the britches. There was a cartoon movie called, "The Little Rascals," where these three little guys got into trouble and put books in their britches so the spanking wouldn't hurt so much. Snap thought it might work, so we tried it.

Dad came in our room, closed the door and was not happy. He told us how upset Mom was and asked us why we were wrestling in the living room after she told us to go outside.

We knew what we did was stupid, but we continued to be stupid and said, "Sorry, Dad, we forgot."

"You forgot? Okay, you're going to get a spanking to help you not forget again."

Dad sat down on the end of the bed with his knees together and said, "Okay, who's first?"

Snap said, "I'll go."

He lay belly-down across Dad's knees and, just as Dad was about to administer a well-deserved spanking, he stopped. Tapping the bottom of Snap's britches with his index finger, he asked, "What's this?"

Snap answered, "A book."

"That's one of the oldest tricks in the book. Now, take it out."

Dad was smiling a little bit as Snap stood up, reached back and pulled out a thin, hardcover book and handed it to him. Dad looked at it and said, *"Snow White and the Seven Dwarfs.* Good book, but there's nothing *Snow White* about you two. Okay Snap, let's get this over with."

Snap did as he was told and once again, before he began the spanking, Dad tapped on the back of his jeans. He tapped again, tried to hide a smile, and then told Snap to stand up. He asked if there was another book in his britches and Snap fessed up and said, "Yes."

Dad said, "Okay, hand it over." Snap reached back and pulled out another book. Dad examined it and said, "*The Hardy Boys*, now there's a couple of *good* boys."

We didn't understand what he meant when he was talking about *Snow White*, but we did figure out the point he was making with the *Hardy Boys*. He read us all the *Hardy Boys* books and those two boys solved a lot of mysteries and crimes in their hometown, so they were really good guys. We think he was comparing us to the *Hardy Boys*.

Dad didn't seem real mad anymore, but he asked Snap if he had more books in his britches and he said, "No, just a magazine."

"Give it to me."

Snap handed Dad the magazine. He looked at it, smiled broadly and said, "This is one of my *TIME Magazines*. What's it doing here?"

"It's an old one and we brought it up here just in case."

"Just in case what?"

"You know ..."

"Then Dad mumbled something about, "Oh, Good Lord ..."

Then he asked me, "Okay John, do you have books in your britches?"

I told him I only had one and it was a fat one because Snap put all the skinny ones in his britches. Dad put his hand out and said, "Let's see it."

I handed it to him and he read the title––*The Adventures of Tom Sawyer and Huckleberry Finn.* He started laughing really, really hard. As a matter of fact, he was laughing so hard he took his glasses off and wiped his eyes with his hanky. We didn't know what was so funny, but we laughed just because Dad was laughing.

When Dad finished laughing, he stood up, pointed the book at us and said, "PERFECT!"

Then he dropped the book on the bed and walked towards the door when Snap asked, "Aren't you going to give us a spankin'?"

He stopped, turned towards us and said, "I should. But I can't."

That didn't make any sense to us, but we were sure happy we dodged another bullet. At least, at the time, we thought we had. He then said, "Now, you boys stay in your room until we call you down for supper. No wrestling, no fighting, no noise––no nothing! Understand?"

"Yes, Dad."

It was boring. We wanted to wrestle, but didn't. We shoved each other around a little bit, but that was it. We talked about taking our BB guns out from under the bed, opening a window and blasting some sparrows and blackbirds. But, if Dad caught us he'd take our guns away, so we let that one go, too. So we just lay around, lit a few farts and talked about old people who smelled funny.

We were really getting hungry. It was 6:30, but Mom and Dad hadn't called us for supper yet. I went to the top of the stairs and yelled down, "Me and Snap are starving! When is supper?"

Dad appeared at the bottom of the stairs and said, "Boys, we've just finished supper and there's nothing left."

I pleaded with him and said, "But Dad, you said you and Mom would call us when it was time for supper, why didn't you call us?"

"SORRY BOYS, WE FORGOT!"

Chapter 6

BONK!

"Hole in the Head"

Dateline: Early 1950s

One cold winter Saturday, me and Snap were down in the basement just messin' around. Mom came to the top of the steps and announced that Bronko and his mom were coming over. That was great news! Bronko was a couple years older than us and a lot bigger and stronger, but he was a super guy and we had fun doing stuff with him.

We loved to wrestle Bronko because he was a tough challenge. We could get him down sometimes and could never make him give, but now we had another opportunity!

We planned an ambush and a booby trap. We opened the door to our playroom just a little bit and placed a two-by-four board on top of the door frame. Our plan was almost perfect!

Snap was standing inside the door so Bronko could see him. I was standing on a chair behind the door.

When Bronko pushed the door open and stepped in, the two-by-four would fall flat and horizontally, just dinging him on the head a little. When that happened, Snap would tackle him low around the legs and I'd jump off my chair onto his back. This would bring him down to the floor––then we'd make him give! That was the plan.

It wasn't long before Bronko came running down the stairs, but he didn't come in. He stood outside the door and said, "Let's go outside and play!"

"We will go out in a little bit, but first come on in!"

"I'm going outside, guys. I'll see you out there."

"Come on Bronko, we just want to show you something before we go outside."

"Later boys, I'm going outside."

Doggone it. What went wrong? Why didn't he come in? No one knew about our trap but me and Snap. We just couldn't figure out why he didn't come in. Well, in a few minutes, Mom hollered down, "Boys, Bronko is going outside! Now, get up here right now and go outside and play!"

You could always tell when Mom wasn't happy and she meant business and this was one of those times when she meant business. So, brainlessly and without further thought, I jumped off the chair and headed out the door.

BONK!!!!!!!

The next thing I remembered was being on my hands and knees. Mom was wiping blood off both sides of my head and dabbing at a hole in the top of my head. Bronko stood there telling everyone, "I didn't go in that room because I saw that two-by-four on top of the door."

I wanted to talk, but I was too dazed. I was just trying to figure out what happened. Obviously, I must have gotten BONKED by my own booby trap! That part of the deal wasn't in our plans! Me and Snap weren't always the brightest bulbs on the tree, and this is one of the dim light-bulb moments!

Mom walked me out to the car and we headed downtown to the Carroll Clinic. We were taken into one of those examination rooms and Dr. Walter Anneberg came in. As he sat down next to me and began probing my wound, he asked Mom, "What in the heck happened?"

She simply said, "I think you should ask John."

So he did, and I told him the truth. Then he said, "So, let me get this straight. You set the booby trap for Bronko, but you forgot and walked out the door and it went off on you! Is that right?"

"I guess."

When I said that, he started coughing and wheezing, and then he left the room. I looked at Mom and she was laughing.

I asked her why Dr. Anneberg left the room.

"I think he had to compose himself."

Well, I didn't know what "compose" was, but I figured out it had something to do with that ...

HOLE IN MY HEAD!

Chapter 7

FORTS IN THE JUNGLE

"Pukin' from the Tree Tops"

Dateline: 1950 through 1955 – Ages 5 to 10

The "Jungle" started about one hundred yards east of our house, running north and south for about three city blocks. There was a wide open area in the middle of the Jungle about the size of a football field, and the rest of it was, well, Jungle. There were trees and more trees. We climbed all of them and fell out of most of them.

The Jungle was one of our favorite playgrounds. We spent many a day there, and even some nights. We played ball there, chased wild critters there, knocked monkeys out of trees there (Snap, our friends and I were the monkeys), and built forts there. Our forts were a thing of beauty. They were huge piano boxes that we purchased from Mr. Wagner, who just lived up the street from us. He sold pianos for a living. Five bucks a box and we were the proud owners of two of them. No mortgage; we owned them free and clear.

Our fort was two stories high. We stacked one box on top of the other. The first floor was where we stored our food, BB guns, comic books and toilet paper. Yes, we did a lot of poopin' and peein' in the Jungle, so we needed that stuff. The fort's second floor was our war room and bedroom. We painted pictures on the walls and laid some old carpet on the floor. It was the neatest fort on the planet.

Our neighborhood of kids was about ten square blocks and there were dozens of kids our age and a bunch of kids a few years older. We were all mostly friends, but for the sake of "war games," we formed gangs. The *Bruner Gang,* the *Farner Gang,* the *Moen Gang,* the *Stoffers Gang,* the *Wilson Gang,* and a few other gangs from outside our turf. Most of the time, the *Farner Gang* and the *Bruner Gang* were allies. As a matter of fact, Cy Farner helped us buy, build and defend our fort. He was our good buddy; we could always depend on Cy.

When the gangs got together, we wrestled, boxed (each of us had a pair of boxing gloves), had pea-shooter fights, slingshot battles (these were dangerous), and tree-climbing challenges (two guys climbed the same tree; then kicked, pushed, slugged and stomped on each other's feet and hands until one guy was knocked out of the tree).

Occasionally, some bad blood developed and threats were exchanged. One such threat came from an opposing gang member who Snap knocked out of the tree. He told us he would be back and destroy our fort. We made it very clear to him that it would be the biggest mistake of his young life.

A week after this incident, the Bruner and Farner families took off for their annual summer vacation to Lake Okoboji. The two families were very close, and for many years, vacationed together. However, before we left, Snap, Cy and I went to the Jungle to add a little extra protection to our fort. We dug a three-foot tiger trap right in front of the ground floor entrance. We collected some dog dung, dropped it in the bottom of the trap, then covered the trap with sticks and grass. If anyone tried anything while we were gone, they would pay dearly for their aggression!

We had a great vacation, and as soon as we got back, we ran out into the Jungle to check on our fort. We came upon our worst nightmare––our fort was destroyed! As a matter of fact, it was torched––burned to the ground! Our blood was boiling, but we knew one thing for certain; one of those guys got swallowed up by our tiger trap. It was caved in and the stuff on the bottom was flattened against the ground, and did it ever stink!

Remember, we warned those guys what would happen if they attacked our fort. So Snap, Cy and I grabbed our Cub Scout hatchets and a handful of cherry bombs and headed up the jungle trail to destroy the enemy's fort. Their fort was a beauty, just like ours––two stories and sturdy. When we arrived, no one was there.

We quickly went about our business. Snap and I worked on the side walls, and Cy climbed up on the roof and jumped up and down until it caved in. We were doing this during broad daylight, so we needed to finish it and get out of there. We packed our gear, lobbed a few cherry bombs into what was left of the fort, and retreated to the safety of our turf. Wow, we really did a job on that fort! The cherry bombs started it on fire and we could see it burning two blocks away.

That evening the phone rang and Dad spent about ten minutes talking to someone. When he got off he said, "Boys, up to your room; we need to have a talk."

I hated it when he said that!

As it turned out, the person on the phone was the grandma of the boy whose fort we destroyed. She was in the kitchen at the time of our raid and she watched the entire event. Dad asked, "Did you do it?"

"Yes, but he destroyed our fort first."

Dad told us that the other boy told his folks he *didn't* destroy our fort.

We said, "Dad, you are a lawyer; let's have a trial, because he's a liar!"

Well, as it turned out we had to buy that liar two new piano boxes. That was a bad deal and now we were broke. We walked back into the Jungle and tried to let go of some of our anger and disappointment when, out of the blue, Snap said, "John, I have a great idea, let's build our new fort there."

He was pointing to the biggest tree in the jungle. Yes, a fort in the tree. It was a great idea––Snap was a smart guy!

There were a lot of new houses being built in our neighborhood, so we decided to borrow some of their lumber. When the builders left at the end of the day, we would pick up the discarded nails and wood and haul it over to our tree. We built a great tree fort in the Jungle with a window to the north, a window to the south, and a trap door on the floor so we could get in and out of the fort. We accidentally built the fort at a slant, so it was hard to stand up in it. We loved it anyway and supplied it with crackers, comic books, our *Daisy Red Ryder* BB guns, toilet paper, sling shots, a bucket of rocks, a bucket of water, a bucket of sand and, just for good measure, a couple of Swisher Sweet cigars. I won't tell you how we got those cigars, but when we tried to smoke them, we got so sick we were both hanging out the windows, "pukin' from the tree tops." Talk about sick!

Oh, the buckets. The rocks were for our slingshots, the water was dumped on invaders trying to climb up to our fort, and the bucket of sand followed the water. When those guys were wet, the sand really stuck to them! After we soaked and sanded them, you should have heard them swear at us. Their favorite description of us was, "You little sonsab _ _ _ _ es!"

They gave us the finger while firing their slingshots and BB guns into the windows of our fort. Those guys couldn't take a joke!

One time when Snap and I were in our tree fort, four guys a couple of years older than us approached our fort, spoiling for a fight (surprise, surprise). We asked them what they wanted and their response was, "We want you two little chicken sh _ _ s to come down and fight."

Chicken sh _ _ s? That was a pretty cool swear word! We liked it, so we challenged them back with their own words, "Come up and get us, you chicken sh _ _ s!"

AND THE BATTLE WAS ON!

Chapter 8

COONSKIN CAPS

Dateline: 1955-56

Davy Crockett (played on TV by Fess Parker) ... we loved that guy and wanted to be just like him. I can still hear and sing that great Ballad of Davy Crockett.

> *"Born on a mountain top in Tennessee,*
> *Greenest state in the land of the free.*
> *Raised in the woods so he knew every tree,*
> *kilt him a b'ar when he was only three.*
> *Davy, Davy Crockett, king of the wild*
> *frontier."*

That's one of my favorite songs of all time. I still know all the words. But, greater than the song, was Davy's coonskin cap. I can still see ol' Davy with his coonskin cap on; and his sidekick, George Russell, riding into the Alamo to fight in one of the most epic battles in American history.

Me and Snap and most of the guys bought coonskin caps and wore them all the time, except in school and church. We tried to wear 'em to bed a few times, but Mom always came in and took them away from us. She knew if she didn't, we'd just put them back on when she left the room. Man, we loved those coonskin caps.

Mom frequently complained about how bad they smelled, but we couldn't smell anything bad. As a matter of fact, we kinda liked the way they smelled.

I remember one hot summer day me and Snap came in for lunch and Mom said, "My God boys, those caps stink terrible! Take them off and give them to me."

"How come, Mom?"

"Because I'm going to wash them! I can't stand the smell anymore."

We were not happy campers about it, but handed them over to Mom. She put them in the kitchen sink, poured some Tide crystals over them, then ran hot water in the sink. Oh my gosh, did it smell! It's the first time me and Snap realized they stunk. We couldn't figure how come they got so smelly.

Mom worked those things up and down, back and forth and kept her head turned away from the sink. For ten minutes, the only thing she said was, "PEW! OH, PEW!"

When she finished, Mom put those things in a white towel. Big mistake! The towel turned a funny looking brown. We didn't say anything because we knew she wasn't happy.

She took our treasured coonskin caps down to the basement and came back up empty-handed.

"What did you do with them, Mom?"

"I put them in the furnace room to dry out."

"Why didn't you just put them outside in the sun?"

"If I would have put them outside in the sun every cat, dog, and coyote in Carroll County would be in our back yard trying to eat those stinky things."

She laughed. We laughed. Mom was cool.

It only took a couple of days for those caps to dry out, but it seemed more like a couple of weeks to me and Snap.

Mom and Dad were the only ones who could take our coonskin caps. If anyone else tried to take them, or anyone else bad-mouthed them, they needed to get ready to rumble. Those coonskin caps were our pride and joy. They were almost sacred.

Not many messed with our coonskin caps, but one hot summer day a kid who was a couple years older than us came walking down the jungle trail. He was a fat kid who lived about three blocks away and he didn't cause any trouble until this day.

Me and Snap and Cy Farner had our coonskin caps on and we were just hanging around our jungle fort. It was our Alamo and we were about to defend it. The kid's name was

Ron, and he came on our turf spoiling for a fight. It surprised us. He normally was a good kid.

"What are you guys doing?"

"Oh, just messin' around."

"Why are you wearing those stupid coonskin caps? It's 90 degrees; what's the matter with you guys? Are you idiots?"

"Watch your mouth, Ron, unless you want to eat your words."

"Oh, those coonskin caps really make you tough. Which one of you is the real Davy Crockett?"

"Get out of here, Ron!"

"Kiss my butt, Davy Crockett."

"What did you say?"

"I said, KISS MY BUTT! If you didn't have those ugly coonskin caps down around your ears, you could hear me!"

He just crossed the line. Too bad for the fat boy with the big mouth because ...

'THEM WAS FIGHTIN' WORDS!

Chapter 9

KILLED IN THE FORT

"Me & Lazarus"

Dateline: Summer 1954

Me, Snap, and Cy Farner built a new fort in the Jungle. It was different than our other forts because we had a foxhole under this one. We sawed the bottom off of a piano box and placed it over the foxhole. The foxhole was about 2½ feet deep, so we could almost stand up inside. That was one cool fort!

In the late afternoon one day, we were out messing around in the Jungle when Cy's older brother, Steve, showed up. He was a good guy and we liked him, but once in a while he was known to stir up a little trouble.

Anyway, Steve was interested in the fort so we all crawled in. Cy made the mistake of bragging to his brother that our fort had very strong walls, so no rocks or BB gun shots could break through!

Well, Big Steve accepted that information as a challenge, and ordered us to stay inside. He'd go out and throw a few rocks at it.

We were good with that.

We were positive that no rock could penetrate those walls. Steve started peppering the east wall of the fort with what sounded like little rocks. Cy and I were inside laughing as we listened to the rocks.

Ping!

Ping!

Zing!

Ding!

Zing!

Ping!

Ping!

One after another, they ricocheted off the outside walls. This was great fun until, all of a sudden, there was a HORRIFIC explosion inside the fort!

It killed me instantly! Steve had launched a small boulder through the east wall of the fort, and it struck me on the right side of my forehead and eye.

I didn't have a chance. My life had been snuffed out! There I was, lying dead on the floor of our jungle fort. I knew I was dead because I wasn't moving. I couldn't see anything and I didn't feel any pain. I often heard Dad and Mom talk about people who died. It seemed like they would always say, "Well, he isn't suffering anymore. His pain is over."

That was me. No pain. I WAS DEAD!

I had never died before, so I found out some things about dead people. First of all, even though they are dead, they can still hear. I could hear Cy and Steve yelling at each other, using some rather colorful words in the process. I gotta confess that me and Snap knew a few colorful words ourselves, but not as many as those two Farner boys!

I also found out that dead people's brains keep working, because my brain was still thinking. I felt my brain thinking about things like ... I wonder if anyone will be sad that I died.

Probably not, because I was still pretty little and I think people only cry when old people die.

My brain was also thinking about that stuff they write in the newspaper about dead people.

There wouldn't be much to write about me because I was only ten. It would probably say that my name was John William Bruner and I was born on May 22, 1944. My mom and dad were Mr. and Mrs. Robert Bruner and that I had one sister, Judy, and one brother, Brian, and another brother, Barry, and another kid on the way. I didn't know his or her name yet. Then, it would tell that I went to school at St. Lawrence and played in the Jungle.

THE END.

It would be so short, people could read it in fifteen minutes!

I was also thinking that I hadn't seen God yet, so I figured out that maybe He hadn't decided what to do with me. That worried me, because once I was helping Dad start a fire in the fireplace and I got a little burn on my finger and it really hurt and I remember someone said that a fire in the fireplace is only half as hot as the fire in Hell!

My brain started to worry, so I started praying the *Our Father*.

I was only halfway through my prayer when I felt my hands touch. I had folded my hands. I was coming back to life! I opened my eyes. Well, I only opened my left eye, because my right eye was still closed from that boulder that hit it.

I sat up.

It was a MIRACLE! God brought me BACK TO LIFE!

I was kinda like that old guy in the bible that Sister Donna told us about who was dead for a whole week and Jesus made him alive again. I was only dead for a little while, but it worked the same way, except that the dead guy walked out of the tomb and I was about to crawl out of the fort.

I did crawl out of the fort, and there was Snap and Cy and Steve and Mrs. Farner and Mom and some other neighborhood kids.

When they looked at me, they all kinda groaned because my right eye was so swollen, I looked like a two-headed monster! Mom was brushing me off and examining my eye and Mrs. Farner was really mad at Steve and told him to apologize to me.

He said, "Sorry."

Then Mrs. Farner said, "You didn't mean that. Now say it right!"

Mrs. Farner was a cool mom. She wasn't very big, but when she got mad – watch out!

Steve did what she demanded and said real loud, "I'M SORRY!"

I'm sure he wasn't really sorry, but everyone there kinda laughed because he said it so loud.

After that, we went in the house and Mom made me an ice pack for my eye. While I was in the bathroom holding it on my eye, my sister, Jude Buns, came in and said, "My God! What happened to you?"

Judy was four years older than me, so I knew if I told her the truth, she would understand and believe me. So, I told her the truth ...

"STEVE FARNER KILLED ME!"

Chapter 10

WHERE'S MOM GOING?

"CRAZY"

Dateline: 1952 – Ages 8 & 7

It was late summer and we were in the back yard shooting hoops. Our favorite uncle, Cliffy, showed up and asked, "What are you two little sh _ _ s doing?"

He always called us that name, but we didn't care because other adults called us that, too. So, we just always knew they were talking to us when they said, "Hey, you two little sh_ _s!"

Anyway, Cliffy had some serious business on his mind. He told us that we were driving Mom crazy and if we didn't "shape up" we were going to *Boys Town.*

Boys Town? "What is Boys Town?" we asked him.

He said it was a place where boys went if they were bad. Snap asked, "How bad do you have to be to go there?"

Cliffy said, "As bad as you two are."

I asked him where Boys Town was and he said, "Omaha."

I asked if that was in Carroll and he said, "Hell, no! It's a hundred miles away."

Snap asked him if we were sent there, if we had to stay overnight. We couldn't figure out what was so funny, but Cliffy started laughing really hard. When he stopped laughing he said, "You will be there ten thousand nights."

Well, he started laughing again when Snap asked him if ten thousand nights was as many as a hundred nights.

We couldn't figure out all those numbers that Cliffy was talking about, but it seemed longer than a week and we didn't want to be gone that long. Cliffy reached into his pocket and pulled out two one-dollar bills and said, "Listen, you two have got the 'divil' in you, but if you promise to be good boys and be nice to your mom, I'll give you these. But, you've got to promise."

Hey, it's 1952. A dollar can buy almost anything, even, "a promise to be good." So, we promised!

A couple days later, we were ramming around the house and accidentally broke some stuff. I think it was some special plate that Mom loved, and a lamp in the family room. As a matter of fact, they were both on the same table that we "accidentally" knocked over when we were wrestling.

We could tell that Mom was both sad and mad at the same time.

"Stand right there. Now look at me. I've had it up to here with you two," she said, reaching above her head. "You are driving me crazy! If you don't start being good boys, either *you* will have to go somewhere, or *I* will have to go somewhere. Now, go on; go outside and do whatever you want to do!"

Wow, we really screwed up! Mom was crying. We went next door to Mr. Wagner's house and climbed up on the roof of the south side of his garage. We used to go there a lot because no one could see us there. It was our secret hiding place. We sat down and tried to figure out what Mom just said. We both agreed that we knew where we were going if we continued to be bad––Boys Town!

But, where was Mom going? Would she go somewhere with Dad? Would she go to the neighbors'? Would she go to Uncle Cliff's house? Would she go to Grandma's house in Pocahontas?

That's where she was going, because Grandma was her mom. So, that's what she was saying, "You boys are going to Boys Town or I'm going to Grandma's house."

We got it figured out, and we didn't like it. We decided we were going to be good boys. We went in the house and found

Mom in the kitchen. She looked tired and sad, but we said to her, "Mom, we are going to be good boys forever and ever."

She looked at us and said, "Why are you going to be good boys forever and ever?"

"Because we don't want to go to Boys Town and we don't want you to go to Grandma's. We want you to live with us."

When we said that, her cheeks turned red and her eyes filled up with rain. Then she said, "When I told you that if you don't start being good boys either you will have to go somewhere or I will have to go somewhere, did you think I would send you to Boys Town? Or that I would leave you and move in with Grandma? Is that what you thought?"

We didn't say anything, we just nodded our heads.

Well, we did it again. We made Mom cry. But this time, she wasn't mad at us. We knew she wasn't mad at us, because this time when she was crying ...

SHE WAS HUGGING US!

Chapter 11

MIDNIGHT WITCH

"I gotta pee!"

Dateline: 1949

It was 1949. I was five years old and a pretty normal kid. I had my fantasies and fears, but what happened in the middle of that night is as vivid now as it was sixty years ago when it happened.

Mom said, "John, you just had a bad dream."

"It wasn't a dream, Mom."

"Then you had a nightmare; and a nightmare is a really bad dream that seems like a real event."

"It was real," I insisted, "not a nightmare. Besides, if it was a nightmare, how did the chair at the desk in our room get so close to my bed?"

Mother didn't say anything. She just picked up the chair and put it back by the desk.

Well, this is what Mom said was a nightmare: Me and Snap were sound asleep and it was really late because Mom, Dad and our sister, Judy, were all in bed sleeping. It was totally dark in the house. I woke up because I had to pee. I sat up and was about to get out of bed, when I saw her. There she was, sitting on a chair about three feet away from me. It was a witch. She was dressed all in black with a black veil on her head and funny little glasses.

I was really, really scared. I did the only thing I could think of doing; I started to visit with her. I said, "Hi."

She didn't say anything. She just stared at me. I told her that I was a good boy and that I always ate all my food. She just stared. I told her I could ride my bike and that I liked school. No answer. She didn't even blink. I then told her that Snap was a good boy, too, and that we always do what Mom and Dad tell us to do. No answer. I think she knew the truth. I told her we say our prayers at night and that we love Jesus and that we always brush our teeth in the morning. She didn't care. She just looked at me.

I couldn't hold it much longer. I told her, "I gotta pee!"

The only response was that same steely, scary look. I asked her if I could go to the bathroom now. She just sat there.

Well, this witch was bigger than me and she scared me, so I decided not to try and wrestle her. Instead, I made the same decision that any typical five-year-old would make. I laid back down, rolled over, pulled the covers up, and ... peed my pants ... and ...

WET THE BED!

Chapter 12

TROUBLE IN KINDERGARTEN

"Quicker than a Sister"

Dateline: 1949 – Age 5

It was October, 1949 and I was in my third week of kindergarten at St. Lawrence. My teacher was a nun, and I liked her even though she was really old––maybe 50. She told us when we started the school year that she expected us all to be able to count to 100. That was no big deal; I could count to 100––did it many times at home.

Sister had a nice big, bead board with 10 rows of 10 brightly colored beads. She would call us up to the front of the room and have us count to 100 as she pushed a bead across the board with each number we counted. It didn't seem too hard and each kid did pretty well.

But, now it was my day and my turn. Sister said, "Okay, John Bruner, let's count to 100."

I walked up to her, stood straight, and began to count, "1, 2, 3, 4 ... 29, 30, 31, 32 ... 39, 40, 41, 42 ..."

Holy cow; I drew a blank! What comes after 42?

Sister said, "Okay, let's start over."

I gathered myself and got off to a good start. "1, 2, 3, 4, 5 ... 34, 35, 36, 37, 38, 39, 40, 41, 42."

Panic! It happened again. Why can't I get past 42?

Sister was irritated and I was scared. She said, "I'm going to give you one more chance, and if you don't do it this time you will have to stay after class and count to a hundred for the 2nd graders."

I was in the half-day morning kindergarten class and when the morning was over, the big 2nd graders came in and used our room for the afternoon. The 2nd graders were older and bigger, and I didn't like them. As a matter of fact, I hated them because I knew they would laugh at me. Sister said, "Okay, John, one last chance."

I fired off the first 35 with exceptional speed, but now it was 36 ... 37 ... 38 ... 39 ... 40 ... 41 ... 42 ... Didn't have a clue what came after 42!

Sister said, "Go sit down. You will stay and count for the 2nd graders."

That was the worst moment of my life. I felt sick. I had to get out of there, and I did. As Sister turned her back and started to walk back to her desk, I bolted for the door. No more kindergarten for me––**I QUIT!** Sister saw me and said, "John William, you come back here!"

Now, just so you understand the lay of the land, our kindergarten class was in the basement of the school and so was the lunch room, so when you walked out of our room, you were in the lunch room.

Here I am sprinting through the lunch room, with Sister in close pursuit. I knew if I ran straight away she would catch me, so I took a sharp cut to the left and headed around some lunchroom tables. She chased me, but I could run in circles faster then she could. She stopped, leaned on the table across from me and said, "Now, don't move! I'm coming over there and we are going to walk back into the classroom together. *Don't move!"*

I stood real still until she got about two steps from me––then blasted out of there! Here we go again, round and round those lunchroom tables. I liked to run. This was starting to be fun. I wondered if we were playing, but when I looked at her, she didn't look like she was playing. She stopped again. She didn't look too good. She was huffin' and puffin' and could hardly talk. I stopped and looked across the table at her. She said, "**Don't move!**"

She started walking towards me. "**Don't move!** If you do, I'll call your mom and dad!"

I was only five, but I'd heard that many times before.

I was trying to be a good little dude. I did as Sister told me. I didn't move until she reached out to grab me––then I shot out of there. She didn't chase me. She only hollered, "John William, you are in serious, serious trouble."

As I ran up the stairs and out the school, I hollered back, "So are you!" As I was running home, I couldn't wait to tell Mom how mean Sister was.

We only lived three blocks from school, so it didn't take me long to get home. As I ran up the driveway, I was surprised to see Mom standing on the front porch. I was so happy to see her, I threw my arms around her and said, "Mom, I hate kindergarten! Sister is mean, so I quit!"

I knew something was wrong. Mom wasn't hugging me back. She grabbed me very tightly by the arm and we walked all the way back to school. That whole trip back was a blur, but Mom was talking the entire way, and it wasn't happy talk.

When we got back, the kindergarteners were gone and those big 2nd graders were in my room. Mom handed me over to Sister then left. She didn't even say goodbye, good luck, or nothing. Boy, talk about going it alone––and I was only five.

There had to be 30 of those big 2nd graders in there and Sister said, "Children, today we are going to start our class with John Bruner. He is in kindergarten and he is going to count to 100 for us."

She grabbed her bead board, elevated it, and stood between the door and me. The escape route had been cut off. There were no windows, and I knew if I tried to wrestle Sister I'd go to Hell. So, I had to count and all those hated 2nd graders were glaring at me.

Sister said, "Here we go," and she pushed the first bead across.

I was frozen with fear but I said, "1, 2, 3, 4, 5 ... (I was getting light-headed) ... 6, 7, 8, 9, 10 ... (my tongue felt stiff) ... 11, 12, 13, 14, 15 ... (my armpits started dripping) ... 16, 17, 18, 19, 20 ... (I was starting to get blurred vision) ... 21, 22, 23, 24, 25 ... (I couldn't move my arms) ... 26, 27, 28, 29, 30 ... (I was about to pee my pants) ... 31, 32, 33, 34, 35 ... (I couldn't breathe) ... 36, 37, 38, 39, 40 ... (I was beginning to lose consciousness) . ... 41, 42 ... (I was dying. I felt my little soul leaving my body. My whole life flashed before me.) Then, suddenly, I heard the number "43." Sister said it!

I opened my eyes and said, "44." She smiled. I'm not dead! "45, 46, 47, 48 ... all the way to 100! All the 2nd graders clapped and cheered and Sister patted me on top of the head. I loved those 2nd graders, and Sister was the nicest teacher in the whole world!

Sister said, "Okay, John, you can go home now!"

I couldn't wait to get home and tell Mom how good I did. I was going to run all the way. As I opened the door to leave, there was Mom and there was Dad. At first I couldn't figure out why they were there. Then I did figure it out. They knew I was smart and they knew I could count to 100 and they just wanted to be there ...

TO CONGRATULATE ME!

Chapter 13

MORE TROUBLE IN KINDERGARTEN

"Kindergarten Dropout"

Dateline: 1950 – Age 4

Snap was one of the youngest kids in Carroll to ever go to kindergarten. Most kids had to be five or six to start kindergarten, but Snap was only four. Mom and Dad must have thought he was pretty smart. Why else would they send a 4-year-old off to school?

Unlike his big brother, he was doing well in kindergarten. He could count to 100, never ran away from Sister, and wasn't afraid of 2nd graders. As a matter of fact, he wasn't afraid of anybody! So, things were going good for ol' Snap 'until one cold, snowy December day.

He arrived at school in the morning, all bundled up in his hat, coat, snow pants, and boots. He took off his hat and coat and sat down on the floor to take his boots off. They were the "five buckle" kind of boots.

Because his hands were cold, he was having trouble unbuckling his boots. A couple of nuns standing close by were smiling at him. Snap noticed that and didn't like it. He thought they were making fun of him. But he continued to work on those buckles and then he heard those two nuns giggling. He looked up at them and, sure enough, they *were* looking right at him and giggling!

That was it! He'd had enough. He buckled his boots back up, put on his hat and coat, walked right past those giggling sisters, and went home. End of story ...

SNAP DROPPED OUT OF KINDERGARTEN!

Chapter 14

BUSTED!

"Montezuma's Revenge"

Dateline: September, 1951 – Ages 7 & 6

We loved fruit. We ate it year round and feasted on it in the fall of the year. Our neighborhood was loaded with apple trees, pear trees, and even a beautiful, beautiful grapevine. It was all there for the pickin'––literally!

One warm September Friday evening, we decided to take our little red wagon and go on a "fruit raid." We told Mom and Dad we were just going to go down to the end of the block and that we'd be home soon. They said okay and I told Snap to hop in the wagon and I'd pull him for a ways so the folks wouldn't suspect anything.

We were only a block away from home and it was just about dark, so we had to work fast. Our first visit was to Mr. and Mrs. Martin's grapevines. We snatched four big bunches and moved onto seven or eight different apple trees. We had Dad's flashlight, so we actually climbed a couple of those trees and picked the best ones we could reach. We executed the raid quickly, quietly and efficiently. It went off without a hitch. We had 30-40 apples and those four bunches of grapes. We pulled our loaded little red wagon down an alley and through backyards until we reached the safety of our own yard.

We had a basketball hoop there and Dad hooked up some floodlights so we could shoot around at night. Well, guess what? As we were transporting our stolen merchandise across our backyard, the floodlights suddenly came on!

BUSTED!

Guess who was waiting there to greet us? Guess who almost pooped their pants? Dad asked where we got all the fruit and we told him, "The neighbors' trees."

"Did you ask the neighbors if you could have it?"

"We forgot."

Mom wondered what we were going to do with all that fruit and we told her we were going to eat most of it and give her some of the apples to make a pie. That didn't work because she still seemed really mad at us. She did say, however, "Boys, you eat so much fruit now, you have Montezuma's Revenge (diarrhea) most of the time. If you eat all of this, we'll have to put a *cork* in you!"

Mom made us laugh.

Then Dad said, "Boys, there is nothing funny about this. Tomorrow morning you are going to take all this fruit back and tell the neighbors you are sorry and you will never do it again. Now up to bed! Wait a minute, where is my flashlight?"

Even though we got busted big time we still slept pretty good. Mom fixed us a nice breakfast then sent us on our way. As we were pulling our wagon down the sidewalk, we noticed that Mom was still standing there. She probably wanted to be sure we weren't going to eat any of that fruit.

We went to Mr. and Mrs. Martin's house first and we didn't even have to knock because she was standing at the door. It was almost as if she knew we were coming. Mr. and Mrs. Martin were old people, but they were really nice––especially Mrs. Martin. We told Mrs. Martin, "We took some of your grapes last night and forgot to ask you and we are sorry. We brought all the grapes back and didn't eat any of them."

Mrs. Martin said, "Thank you for telling me this. My husband and I really like you boys and we want you to have these grapes and all the grapes you want. All you have to do is ask us whenever you want them."

We promised, thanked her, and then went to the other neighbors. Can you believe it? No one wanted their apples back. They all told us we could keep the apples and thanked us for coming to their house and telling them what we had done. Even though we were little guys, we were starting to get this whole thing figured out.

So, here we are, just about back home, pulling our little red wagon still full of all the fruit that we started out with and there was Mom. She hadn't moved. She was still standing there in the same place she was when we left to return the fruit. As we pulled our wagon up close to her, her arms were still folded and she said, "Did you talk to all the neighbors?"

"Yes."

"Why do you still have all the fruit?"

"They wanted us to keep it."

Then she said, "Boys, every time something good or bad happens in our lives, there is a lesson to be learned. What lesson did you learn today?"

Our answer was about as simple as we were, "We learned that if you steal stuff from someone and you tell them you were stealing their stuff, they tell you that they like you. And then they say ...

"THANK YOU!"

Chapter 15

FRIDAY NIGHT FIGHTS

"Blood & Popcorn"

Dateline: 1948-1955

Friday nights were special!

Around 7:00 to 7:30 p.m., me and Snap and Dad – and sometimes Toad – would go up to the Boys' Room and wrestle. Lumpy wasn't there because he was still a twinkle in Dad's eye. After we finished, we'd head down to the kitchen. Dad always made the popcorn and the boys would make the Kool-Aid. When it was all ready, we'd take it into the family room and gulp it down while watching *Greatest Fights of the Century* sponsored by the Gillette Shaving Company. It was boxing at its best, and more importantly, "fun times with Dad" at their best!

Friday Night Fights – we couldn't wait! It was the best of times and it was our special time alone with Dad. *NO GIRLS ALLOWED!*

We all knew the rules:

- No Slugging
- No Kicking
- No Biting
- No Crying

If anyone violated any one of those rules, the fight's over.

When we'd gather in the Boys' Room for these *Friday Night Fights*, it would always start with Dad getting on his knees, taking his shirt off, and showing us his muscles. We would then tear off our shirts and show him our skinny little muscles. Oh, how I wish I had a picture of that!

The fights were wild and furious. It was the boys against Dad. We'd jump him, try to get him on his back, pin his shoulders down, and declare our victory.

But, it never happened. He'd normally stack us on top of each other and ask if we'd "give up."

Never!

We never gave up and Dad never gave up. We'd get headlocks on him, arm bars, and leg locks, but he'd never say, *"Give!"*

This was not a sissy, powder-puff wrestling match. There was no faking or fraud, like professional wrestling matches. This was the real deal and there were no "timeouts" unless someone got a bloody nose or lip.

Brother Toad got in on a few of these fights, but he was pretty young and didn't quite understand the rules. You know the rules: No slugging, no kicking, no biting, no crying – well, Toad violated all of them! But, the big problem was he was slugging, kicking, and biting me and Snap. He thought we were hurting Dad, so he tried to put a hurt on us! We'd send him flyin' and cryin' and then Dad would call a timeout.

We were reminded that Toad was a lot littler than us and we had to tell him we were sorry. We would show Dad Toad's fang marks in our backs, but he showed us no sympathy. We still had to apologize to that *back-bitin'* Toad.

As the fight grew in intensity, Dad would loft me and Snap high into the air and onto one of the beds. Most of the time, it was a soft landing, but occasionally we would bounce off the bed onto the floor.

"OUCH!"

Dad always asked if we were okay, and he always got his answer as we came off the floor charging into him like raging bulls (or 'calves' in our case).

One night we were really getting rowdy and Dad kept launching us onto the bed. Man, it was great fun! However, the fun stopped when Snap's bed broke and crashed to the floor with a resounding *THUD!*

That wasn't the only time we broke a bed wrestling, and Mom knew it. She came to the foot of the steps and hollered, "Bob, did anyone get hurt?"

"No, Lovey!"

"Did you guys break another bed?"

"It's okay, Lovey! I can fix it."

"Bob, you've got to stop all this rough-housing with the boys. If you don't, they'll grow up to be a bunch of roughnecks!"

"Don't worry, Lovey ...

"THAT WILL NEVER HAPPEN!"

Chapter 16

MONSTERS & SISSIES

"Give 'Em Hell, Lovey"

Dateline: Summer 1954

It was 1954. I was ten and Snap was nine. It was a hot summer day and, as usual, me and Snap were hanging around the front yard looking for a little action. Well, as luck would have it, a couple of new boys in the neighborhood came walking down the sidewalk right in front of our house. We engaged them in some kids' conversation and then asked them if they wanted to wrestle. They were guys about our age and size so, before they could answer "yes" or "no," Snap and I started wrestling with them.

We had rules of engagement back then. First of all, no slugging, no biting, no scratching, no kicking, no name calling, and no swearing! When you were wrestling someone and they said, "Give" or started crying, the match was over and you let them up.

More of and the Best of Me & Snap

Me and Snap weren't the toughest guys on the planet. We'd win some, lose some, cry out, "GIVE!" sometimes, and even occasionally cry, but we enjoyed every encounter. We were kids and it was fun.

We never did ask these kids their names, but we could tell they were good guys because they were wrestling by the rules. We thought we were having fun. Then someone yelled, "HOG PILE!" That's when everyone just piles on top of everyone else. Well, one of the new kids was on the bottom and he started to cry.

We unpiled and immediately said, "Sorry."

Well, they didn't care if we were sorry or not. He and his brother took off running down the street. It was not our intent to hurt anybody – we were just having fun in the Hog Pile! Heck, we did it every day!

We were talking about heading into the Jungle when, all of a sudden, we started playfully wrestling each other. I'm not sure how long we were wrestling, but out of the blue, this adult lady and those two boys were standing right next to us. We jumped up and said, "Hi!"

The lady said, "Don't start acting nice! You started a fight with my boys and almost broke Jimmy's neck! What are you, animals?"

Well, thank God, Lovey (that was Mom's nickname) saw all the commotion and arrived on the scene just in time. She asked the boys' mom what the problem was, and this lady flew off the handle! "We are new in the neighborhood and your boys started a fight with my boys and hurt Jimmy's neck!"

Mom looked at us and said, "Is that true boys?"

We told her we were just having fun wrestling and got in a Hog Pile and didn't mean to hurt anyone. Mom accepted that and told the angry lady we were good boys and that she was sorry that her son got hurt.

This lady was still in a foul mood. "You're not sorry and your boys aren't sorry and this better not ever happen again!"

I'll tell you what – that lady hit Lovey's hot button! Mom took a couple of steps towards her and said, "I think it's time for you to button your lip and go home."

The lady gave Lovey a cautious look then said, "Come on, boys. Let's go!" And, as she was walking away she turned abruptly and said, "Those two boys of yours are a couple of monsters!"

With a lightning response, Mom hollered back, "If my boys are a couple of monsters ...

"YOUR BOYS ARE A COUPLE OF SISSIES!"

(WOW, Mom!)

Chapter 17

SQUIRT GUNS

"Smash"

Dateline: 1955 – Ages 10 & 11

Squirt guns were a marvelous invention. We all carried one in our back pocket or belt all through the 50s. They weren't very big and didn't hold much water, but when we added a couple drops of liquid dish soap or cheap perfume ... WOW, they packed a punch!

Mom made it real clear to me and Snap and our gun-totin' friends that there would be no squirt guns in our house. Her rules were simple:

#1 No loaded squirt guns in the house.

#2 No loading squirt guns in the house.

#3 No squirting squirt guns in the house.

Most of the time, we abided Mom's rules. There was, however, one hot summer day when we thought Mom was gone. Five of us loaded our guns in the kitchen and began soaking each other at close range. In one fell swoop, we had just violated all of Mom's rules. We were loud and messy and having a wild time, when out of nowhere appeared ... you guessed it––MOM. She was not a happy camper.

"Okay, boys that's it! Get out in the garage."

We nervously hustled out there and she was right behind us.

"Give me those squirt guns! All of them!"

"Mom, you can't take these guys' guns. They're not ours."

"Listen, any squirt gun in MY house is MY gun. Now hand them over. That includes you too, Cy, and Steve, and Pat."

That ended any debate. We all handed them over.

Mom took the five guns, laid them in a nice straight row, took Dad's hammer out of the toolbox and––smash, smash, smash, smash ... SMASHED them all!

Then she swept the pieces together with her hands and smashed the pieces to pieces.

She wasn't done yet. She swept those pieces together again and then smashed the pieces of the pieces to pieces.

That was it, we got the message! Boy did we ever get the message!

"Mom, can we have all those pieces?"

"Why?"

"Snap said he thinks he can glue them back together."

The guys laughed quietly and there was a tiny smile on Mom's face. That made us feel good because the way she was smashing those guns I thought she hated us.

"Alright boys, get on your bikes and go for a long ride. You have too much energy and you need to burn it off. Now, get out of here before I lose my temper."

"Mom, the way you were smashing those guns ..."

"That's enough––get going!"

"Okay, Mom, see you later."

"Can't wait!"

I don't think she was serious. But anyway, we hopped on our bikes and headed for town––downtown that is. We needed to ...

BUY SOME SQUIRT GUNS!

Chapter 18

PIGEON PIE & PIGEON POOP

"Just Little Guys"

Dateline: 1954 – Ages 10 & 9

When we were just little guys, a nice girl by the name of Lorraine Wiederin lived with us during the week to help Mom. It was wild around our house, and Mom needed all the help she could get. Lorraine lived on a farm five miles north of Carroll. Every Saturday, the folks gave her a ride home and Snap and I would always ride along.

One Saturday she asked if we would like to spend the rest of the weekend on the farm with her mom, dad, brother Ralph, and herself. We begged Mom and Dad to let us stay. They didn't hesitate a bit to say yes (surprise, surprise). They needed frequent breaks from us two little guys.

What a weekend; it was a blast! We rode their plow horses, caught real live, beautiful pigeons, peed and pooped in a real outhouse, got to touch a real electric fence, wrestled Mr. Wiederin, ate pigeon pie, slept in a down-filled feather bed, and on Sunday, went to Mass at a real country church in Mount Carmel. It was a fantastic experience. We had become country boys; and we loved it!

After that, we spent every weekend we could on the farm. The Wiederins were such wonderful people, who seemed genuinely happy to have us stay with them. We even rode our bikes out there on some Saturdays, spent the day and rode back home in the late afternoon. It was a hard five mile ride on gravel roads and we were little guys who got hot, tired and stinky. But we didn't care!

Snap and I were fascinated with pigeons. We caught them in the barn and Mrs. Wiederin would clean and cook them for us. And sometimes we'd bring them home and Mom would cook them. Man, oh man, were they ever good! Pigeon stew. Pigeon pie. Pigeon cooked any way was our favorite food.

After several months of catching and eating these beautiful birds, we decided to raise them. Mom and Dad were not too happy about this, but gave us permission to raise "a few." We went down to the Fareway Grocery store and the nice manager, Mr. Singsang, gave us some large wooden fruit crates. We put some chicken wire over the front of them, and bingo––we had our pigeon houses!

Dad took us out to the Wiederin farm a couple of nights so Lorraine and Ralph could help us catch just the ones we wanted. It was easy to catch them. Just point the flashlight at them in the barn. They would freeze or fly into the wall. We grabbed them, bagged them and took them to their new home. We wanted only the most beautiful of the pigeons––the white ones and the brown ones.

We had a dozen pigeons. We loved them and they grew to love us, too. We gave them all names. The prettiest white pair we named *King* and *Queen*. We had caught one of their little white babies, also. She was a beauty and we named her *Junior*.

The most striking pair we had was brown and white. The male we named *Cong,* and the female, *Lady*. They really loved each other; they were always side-by-side with their wings touching.

We really, really loved our pigeons. We would run home after school, open their cages and they would fly out and sit on the roof of the house for a few minutes. Then they would fly down and sit on our shoulders, heads, or hands––any place they could find to sit on us. And even though we knew they were lovin' us up, in their excitement, they would poop on us. And, we didn't even care! They were our pets. They were our friends. And I'll say it again––we really loved them.

However, a problem soon developed. Our pigeons flew around after school until it got dark, then flew back into their cages. Before we went to bed each night, we went out to close and lock the cage doors so no predators could get them. But we began to notice there were more than just our white and brown ones in our pigeon houses. There were blue ones. Lots and lots of blue pigeons!

At first, we thought it was pretty cool, until our "beautiful dozen" grew to ten dozen and they were flying around the neighborhood pooping on everyone's roof!

Dad was a lawyer at the time, and the County Attorney. One night after work, he told us the neighbors were complaining to the police, so we had to get rid of the pigeons. That night we went into the cages and sacked them all up. All of them. White ones. Brown ones. Blue ones. There must have been 90 to 100 pigeons, and we took them all back to the farm.

The next morning, they were all back sitting on our roof and the neighbors' roofs doing what pigeons do best.

Snap and I knew instinctively that something terrible was going to happen. Dad said we had to get our BB guns and shoot them!

No way! We couldn't do that. We loved them. So, Dad got some high school boys who lived in the neighborhood to shoot and kill all of them. They put them in large potato sacks and threw them into garbage cans––all of them except our "beautiful dozen." As they tumbled to the ground, mortally wounded, we cradled them in our hands and arms to carry them ever so lovingly to their final resting place––our backyard. There we dug a shallow grave, laid them beside their respective partners (with *Cong* and *Lady* pressed tightly together, wing-to-wing, for eternity) covered them with God's warm earth and a couple of Mom's flowers, and stood there. We didn't say any prayers **because we were just little guys.** We didn't tell each other how sad we were, **because we were just little guys.** We just stood there, side-by-side, hung our heads and cried. Because ...

WE WERE JUST LITTLE GUYS!

Chapter 19

YELLOW SNOW

"Jimmy D & Poopy Dog"

Dateline: 1950s

In the 1950s, Carroll, Iowa had a population of 7,000. I know that to be true because that's what Dad told me and Snap, and Dad was a pretty smart guy. Mom was smart, too. That's why me and Snap couldn't figure out why we were so stupid.

Anyway, Carroll's people population was 7,000, but it had another very significant population——dogs. There must have been at least three thousand of those critters! It seemed like almost every house had a dog. There were dogs all over the place! I don't think there were any laws or regulations about dogs back then and, if there were, no one paid any attention to them.

Dogs roamed free all over town and they left their mark. During the summer, all the yards were full of their decorations of thick, dark green clumps of heavily fertilized grass and bright yellow areas of gagging grass. In the winter time, they provided beautiful yellow snow and small mountains of steaming fertilizer. Us guys used to eat a lot of snow, but we didn't eat the yellow snow because our parents told us it could kill us.

I do have to admit, though, we did taste it because we were stupid. But, we didn't die because we just tasted just a little bit of it. To be honest, it really didn't taste much different than the white snow.

Speaking of yellow snow, me and Snap made some of our own yellow snow. But we didn't just make yellow holes, we were artistic. We'd make faces with eyes, nose, mouth and even teeth, if we had enough ammo.

One day, we were making yellow snow faces in the backyard and Mom caught us. She told us to, "Get in the house, right now!" When we got in the house she told us, "Only bad boys pee outside and, besides that, if you do it too often, IT might freeze off."

Freeze off? Good God, what would we do if it froze off? We talked about it and figured out we'd die if THEY froze off, so there were no more yellow faces in the snow for us THAT winter! But, even though we were stupid, we did figure out that Mom was just trying to scare us so we wouldn't do it anymore. Besides, a high school kid told us, "You can't freeze those things off!"

Well, back to the dogs. There were ALL kinds of dogs. Playful dogs, stupid dogs, dancin' dogs, and dead dogs. The playful dogs ran at us and we'd try to catch them in the air. Sometimes, we'd catch them and hug them and sometimes they'd knock us on our butts! The stupid dogs used to chase cars and do other stupid stuff. Like Brian Fitzpatrick's beagle. One day, it was sniffing around our bucket of snapping turtles that we caught at the creek, and one of those little guys snapped onto that old Beagle's ear! Oh, my gosh! That dog ran and howled and ran and howled and ran some more, while six of us were chasing her. We finally caught her in Fitzpatrick's backyard and that little turtle wouldn't let go! We tugged and pulled on that dang turtle while that poor dog screamed to high heaven. Finally, Mrs. Fitzpatrick came out with some salt and poured it on the head of that snapper and it let go. We let the dog up and it took off running and howling. It was so stupid; it thought the turtle was still attached!

Then there were the dancin' dogs. They would run at us and lock their legs around us and dance around and around like we were their partner. We thought it was pretty funny until our high school hero, Kenny Macke, told us what they were really trying to do. Well, we didn't quite "get it" because we didn't know all the "facts of life" stuff. But, even though we were stupid, we knew it was something dirty. So, after that, when they would try dancin' with us, we'd whack 'em, smack 'em and slug 'em until they stopped. When those little mutts would wrap their legs around our ankles and do that same stuff, we'd just boot them high in the air! They'd bellow as they flew through the air and wouldn't stop bellowing until they hit the ground with a THUD!

Now, we never, ever killed any dogs because we loved them all, and because we weren't that kind of kids. But, we did stop them from doing all that dirty crap!

Dead dogs! Okay, there were a lot of dogs and a lot of cars. So, as the old saying goes, "Every puppy has its day." We saw a lot of dogs that got smashed. Unfortunately, one of those dogs was our dog, Daisy, and tragically, Mom was the driver of one of those cars.

Me and Snap and our older sister, Jude Buns, were in the front yard this one summer afternoon, and Mom came driving up the driveway with a carload of groceries. Daisy chased her up the driveway. We all saw what was about to happen and we started waving our arms and hollering at Mom, "STOP! STOP! STOP!"

She didn't get our message and just smiled and waved at us.

Oh crap! Crunch! Crunch! Daisy got smashed by both the front tires and back tires! She was "flatter'n a pancake" and "deader than a doornail."

Mom screamed!

Judy screamed!

Me and Snap screamed!

Mom cried.

Judy cried.

Me and Snap cried.

Mom asked for help.

Jude Buns puked, and me and Snap ... well, we headed for the Jungle.

It was painful to lose our puppy friends, but it seemed like every time we buried one, a new dog would come into our lives. This happened a couple of weeks after Daisy got smashed. We were in Dr. Rease Anneberg's backyard, flipping over big flat rocks and catching the snakes that lived under them, when a new little kid and his dog showed up. I saw him and ran over to talk to him.

"Hi, kid!"

"Hi."

"What's your name?"

"Jimmy D."

"That's a good name. What's your dog's name?"

"Poopy Dog."

"Poopy Dog? How come you named him Poopy Dog?"

"I didn't. My mom did."

"So, why did your mom name him Poopy Dog?"

"Because he poops all the time and he poops everywhere!"

"Does he poop in the house?"

"Yep, and he poops in other people's houses, too. He even poops in the street and he poops on sidewalks and even poops on driveways. He poops everywhere! Mom said it's a good thing he can't fly."

"Your mom is funny."

"Not when she is cleaning up poop, she's not funny."

I hollered over at Snap and the guys and said, "Hey everybody, we have a new kid and a new dog that moved in. This is Jimmy D and Poopy Dog!"

They all ran over and said, "Hi," to Jimmy D, and patted Poopy Dog on the head and the back. We invited him to help us catch snakes and he said, "Naw, I'm only 5 ½. I just like to watch you guys."

One day, we were out in the Jungle messin' around in our fort, and Jimmy D and Poopy Dog showed up. We told him to come in and see our fort, so both he and Poopy Dog ventured in. Well, they couldn't have been in the fort more than a minute and good old Poopy Dog lived up to his reputation. He dumped a load just inside the door and, was it ever rotten! We all got the heck out of the fort. I got as much of that poop out of there as I could. Meanwhile, Jimmy D was on his knees holding Poopy Dog by the ears and scolding him, "You bad dog! You don't poop in the fort! You bad dog! Do you hear me? You bad dog!"

It was so neat! All the time, Jimmy D was chewing out Poopy Dog, Poopy Dog was licking his face, his nose, his mouth. Talk about a love story! Jimmy D and Poopy Dog were the real deal!

Jimmy D and Poopy Dog came around a lot just to watch us guys and see what we were up to. When we'd see them, we would always stop what we were doing and run over and greet them. We loved those two. They made us smile.

Oh yes, growing up in the small town of Carroll was very special and growing up in the 50s was a very special time. And it was always a very special event when we'd be doing our thing and one of the guys would holler out, "Hey everybody, here comes ...

"JIMMY D AND POOPY DOG!"

(Priceless!)

Chapter 20

<u>DUMB & DUMB "OR"</u>

"Smack!"

Dateline: 1951 – Ages 7 & 6

In the fall of 1951, I was in 2nd grade, and somehow Snap made it back into and out of kindergarten and was doing quite well in the 1st grade. My 2nd grade teacher was not young, not happy, not healthy, not nice, and not very considerate of the fact that we kids were only seven years old and not very smart yet. Two weeks into the school year, she thought she knew who the smart ones were, who the average ones were, and who the dumb ones were. The smart kids, she put into the "Blue Group." The average kids were in the "Red Group," and the dumb ones were in the "Yellow Group." I was in the Red Group and I liked it there because there wasn't as much pressure to get all the answers right.

I'm not sure where this teacher came from, but she was slap-happy. Often, if we didn't know an answer or gave the wrong answer, she'd smack us with an open hand on the back of the head or the side of the face. She wasn't very big, but she could sure pack a wallop. I don't think a day ever passed in 2nd grade that she didn't pop a kid or two.

Anyway, one day it was my turn to read out loud to the class a couple of paragraphs from a story about *The Little Engine that Could.* I was moving along really well until I got to the part where the Little Engine was close to the top of the hill. If it had enough power, it would make it over the hill; **or**, if it didn't have enough power, it would roll backwards down the hill. Or something like that. Well, when I got to the "or" part of the story, I read it as "on," and immediately the teacher stopped me. She pointed to the word "or" and said, "What is that word?"

It looked like "on" to me so I said, "On." She said, "That word is not on, it's **or**. Now start from the beginning of the paragraph and get that word right."

Slap-Happy was beginning to make me nervous because she was standing right next to me when she was telling me "that word," and she was tapping me on the top of the head with her finger. I did as I was told and as I got that little engine close to the top––I stopped. There in front of me was "that word." I forgot what she told me, and it still looked like "on" to me. This teacher was losing patience with me. She asked, "What ... is ... that ... word?"

I fell silent. Couldn't talk. Couldn't think. Could hardly see the word anymore. She started tapping me on the head again and said, "You tell me that word right now and I mean **RIGHT NOW!**"

I had to do something or she was going to tap a hole in my head, so I said it as I saw it, "**ON**!"

BAM!!!!!

She smacked me across the face, grabbed me by the ear, pulled me out of my desk, pushed my book into my chest and said, "Go across the hall to the 1st grade and ask your brother what this word is. He's smart."

Well, she didn't say I was dumb, but I was smart enough to know that I was dumb.

I walked over to the 1st grade room and knocked. Sister Donna came to the door and smiled, "What's the matter, John?"

All the kids loved Sister Donna because she loved all the kids and I always liked being around her because she always made me feel good. She was my 1st grade teacher, too. Anyway, I told her I needed to talk to Snap. She said, "Okay," and had Snap come out into the hall. Sister Donna went back into the classroom and Snap asked me what was going on. I told him I needed his help to learn a word. He asked me what word it was. I showed him "that word," he looked at it, and said, "I don't know. I've never seen that word before."

After he said that, he turned and walked back into his classroom. I just stood there. I was sad and I was scared. I had to do something. I thought about bolting out of there and heading home, but that didn't work very well when I was in kindergarten, so I decided not to try it again. I couldn't go back into my classroom if I didn't know "that word," so I was stuck standing outside the 1st grade room.

I was seven years old and my life was crashing in on me from all sides. I was crying a little bit and then all at once Sister Donna was there. She leaned over and cupped my face in her warm hands and said, "What's the matter, John? What happened?"

I told her the story and then ... then ... she put her arms around me and hugged me. I didn't mean to make her sad, but I could tell she was crying. After a little bit, she rubbed my head and said, "Come with me, John. I can help you."

As we walked back into her 1st grade room, I saw her take out a little white hanky and wipe her eyes and nose. I guess she had a cold and I didn't care if I caught her cold because I really liked her.

Sister Donna told the 1st graders, "Class, we are going to learn a new word today and John Bruner is going to help us learn this word."

When she said that, it didn't scare me because she was smiling at me. She went up to the blackboard and wrote in big, big letters the word **FOR.** She looked at me and asked, "John, what is that word?"

I confidently said, "For."

She said, "That's right." Then she took the eraser and wiped off the F. "Now John, what's that new word when we take the F off?"

She made it easy; the answer was "or."

She said, "Very good! Class, John just helped you learn a new word."

When she said that all those little 1st graders started to cheer and clap. I looked around the room for Snap and when I saw him, he was smiling. Everything was okay now. I was ready to go back to my room. I said thank you to Sister Donna. She gave me another little hug and handed me my book, and I walked across the hall to a scary destiny!

When I stepped into the room I was told to sit at my desk, open my story book, and start reading the story from the beginning. Once again, I was cruising right along until I got that "little engine" close to the top of the hill. I slowed down ... my teacher moved closer ... my brain was gasping for oxygen ... and ... there it was ... "that word" right in front of me ... and ... and I didn't know it. I kept trying to think of the word that Sister Donna had written on the blackboard. It was gone. Fear erased it. She was tapping me on the top of my head and telling me, "SAY THAT WORD. SAY THAT WORD."

I didn't know "that word," but I put my arms up beside my face and blurted out, "ON!"

BAM!!!

She smacked me, but it didn't hurt because I blocked it with my arms. She grabbed my ear, pulled me out of my desk, and pushed me to the back of the room. She plunked me down in a desk and said, "You are now in the Yellow Group!"

Well, that made it official. I was dumb. I really didn't feel that bad though because Snap didn't know "that word" either, so we were Dumb & Dumb––thanks to that word––"or." And, you know, at our age, six and seven, we didn't give a hoot.

That evening at the supper table, Dad was quizzing us about our school day. When he asked me how my day was I said, "Okay."

He asked, "Did you learn anything new?"

"Yes, I learned a new word."

"What is that new word?

"I CAN'T REMEMBER!"

Chapter 21

DON'T KILL FRITZ

"Run Away"

Dateline: 1953

Our favorite pet of all time was our little dog, Fritz. She was a Toy Manchester, brown and black, and never weighed more than seven pounds soaking wet. The runt of the litter, we got her for free from our good friends, the Farners. I'm not sure exactly when we got her, but me and Snap were seven or eight years old.

Fritz did everything and went everywhere with us. She was with us in the Jungle, in our forts, at the creek and battled with us as we fought with rival neighborhood gangs. Many of those guys left the battlefield with Fritz's fang marks on their ankles. What a warrior; what a friend. Fritz was a thing of beauty.

As much as we loved Fritz, it didn't take us long to realize that she wasn't the sharpest stick in the pile. In other words, she wasn't real smart. We tried and tried to house-train her, but she never did quite get it. It seemed like Mom was constantly cleaning Fritz's pee out of the carpet. Mom and Dad told us that it was up to us kids to take her outside every morning, noon and night to do her jobs.

We obeyed and did what they told us. She would pee and poop, but it seemed like she always had a little left for the house.

Anyway, one Saturday morning in late September of 1953, we were just rolling out of the sack and I overheard Dad tell Mom, "When I come home at noon, I'm going to take Fritz to get shot."

Oh, my gosh! I ran downstairs to find my dog and there was Mom, kneeling on the dining room floor, cleaning up more of Fritz's pee. I knew that upset Mom and Dad, but I didn't think it was a capital offense.

I ran back up to the Boys' Room, got dressed, brushed my teeth and prepared my strategy to save Fritz. *We had to run away!* That was the only way to save her. Me and Fritz had to run away from home ... far, far away, into the country.

When Mom wasn't around, I snuck into the kitchen, made two peanut butter and jelly sandwiches, filled my Cub Scout canteen with cold water, jumped on my bike, and headed for the country with Fritz in hot pursuit. Only one small problem. In my hurry to get out of the house, I left my canteen in the sink. Darn, it was a hot September day; me and Fritz were going to need water!

I rode hard and fast about ten blocks with Fritz keeping up pretty good. When I stopped to wait for her, we were actually on a gravel road in the country, right next to a tall cornfield. This was a great place to hide! I lifted my bike over the barbed wire fence and then climbed over myself. Fritz just ran under the fence and joined me. We moved about five rows into the corn so we couldn't be seen, but close enough to the road so we could see the passing cars.

Good Lord, it was hot in that old cornfield and we didn't have any water. It was okay though, because we were just sitting down and resting. I'm not sure how long we sat there, but after awhile, I took out the peanut butter and jelly sandwiches. I ate all of mine and Fritz ate most of hers. I finished off the rest of Fritz's sandwich, checked for cars, and then me and Fritz got out of that sticky, hot cornfield and headed north to my good friend Denny Danner's farm.

When we got there, Denny was home and we went into the barn and built a terrific fort from bails of straw. It was great fun and it was a perfect place to hide. I asked Denny if I could have a drink of water. He went in his house and came back with a tall glass of cold water. I drank a bunch, then Fritz drank a bunch. I asked Denny if he wanted some and he just laughed and said, "No."

I was still thirsty, so I finished it off.

We were in the barn quite awhile when Denny's dad came in and said it was time for me to go home because it was getting close to supper time. Me and Fritz headed back to town, but I knew we couldn't go home because I didn't want 'em to kill her. That gravel road was a difficult bike ride and Fritz got so tired that she couldn't go any more. I picked her up and carried her the best I could, but we crashed twice and I ripped my jeans at the knees. Both knees were bleeding a little bit, but I was okay. It didn't hurt that much.

I was really thirsty again and decided I'd go to Cy's house to hide out. Cy was in the backyard and he started laughing when he saw me. I asked him what was so funny and he said, "You're crazy!"

Before we could really start visiting, Cy's dad came out and told Cy to go in the house. I really liked Cy's dad and mom. Mr. and Mrs. Farner were cool parents, just like my mom and dad.

Me and Fritz were sitting in the soft grass and Mr. Farner asked me if I was okay. I told him yes, and about that time Mrs. Farner came running out and asked the same question. She looked worried. I told her I was really thirsty and she hurried back in the house. Mr. Farner knelt down beside me and told me that Mom and Dad were looking for me and that they were really worried. Mrs. Farner came back with a big glass of water. I drank some, Fritz drank some, then I finished it off. Mr. Farner got a big smile on his face and kinda shook his head.

About this time, Mom and Dad came running around the house. She had a wet washcloth and sat right down beside me and hugged me around the neck. Mom was hugging me so hard that I was about choking. As she was wiping my face and arms, she noticed my bloody knees. Mom touched them both with the washcloth and hugged me again. I don't know why she was crying. Maybe she couldn't stand the sight of blood!

"Why did you run away, John?" asked Dad.

"Because, I don't want 'em to kill Fritz."

Dad said, "No one is going to kill Fritz. Fritz is part of the family. We all love Fritz. Why did you think someone was going to kill Fritz?"

"I heard you tell Mom this morning that when you came home for lunch, you were going to take Fritz to get shot."

"John, Fritz has a bad bladder infection. That is why she is peeing so much. I told your mother I was going to take her to get *'A'* shot––not to *get* shot."

Oh, my gosh, I really screwed up! The only thing I could think to say was, *"Sorry."*

Then I asked Mom and Dad, "If someone runs away from home, does that mean he can never go home again?"

Mom was still sitting on the ground next to me, kissing my cheek and rubbing my back. I looked up at Dad and his eyes were full of tears. I knew he wanted to say something because I could see his bottom lip move, but no words came out.

So I asked one more question ...

"CAN I GO HOME?"

Chapter 22

THREE BLOCK FIST FIGHT

"Duel in the Street"

Dateline: 1955 – Ages 11 & 10

It was a hot, late summer afternoon. Snap and I were doing what we did almost every day––wrestling. We were in the front yard, the ground was hard, it was buggy, and we were hot, sweaty and tired. All those conditions caused us to get mad, mean, and stupid. I don't know who threw the first punch, but all of a sudden we were on our feet, standing toe-to-toe, flailing away at each other. Most of our fist fights would only last four or five minutes, no matter whom we were fighting. But this one was a beauty. It lasted twenty minutes and was fought from our front yard to St. Lawrence School––three blocks, or a little more than a quarter of a mile.

Snap was a couple of inches shorter than me, and his style was to always come in low and pound the body, then cut loose with solid uppercuts. My style was to fight backing up, throwing roundhouses to the head and neck. For an exhausting, bruising twenty minutes that's how this battle was fought.

We slugged it out from the front yard, into the street, onto Mrs. Schaefer's north lawn, back into the street, past the Stone's house, into Dr. Anneberg's back yard, then returned to the middle of the street. One block down, two to go. We stopped for a minute or so, caught our breath, called each other some bad names, and then started unloading rights and lefts and uppercuts and roundhouses.

Snap kept coming forward, pounding my midsection and busting my bottom lip wide open with uppercuts. I kept throwing punches to the side of his head and occasionally to his face. His ears were turning black and blue; his right eye was puffy. We fought onto Mr. Martin's front yard, back into the street, into a vacant lot and onto Mr. and Mrs. Frank's front yard. Two blocks down, one to go. We stopped and rested our battered bodies for a little bit.

Snap put his dukes up and said, "Let's go, you fathead."

I was hoping he'd say, "Let's go home," but his, "Let's go" was an invitation to keep on fighting.

So, I obliged him. Back into the street, past the Crouse house, onto the sidewalk, then back across the street. We had just pounded each other for three blocks, and were loading up for number four, when a loud car horn honked at us. Oh, my God! It was Dad and Mom. Dad jumped out of the car and said, "GET IN!"

We got in. Mom was so mad she didn't talk. That ride home seemed longer than the fight.

We were sent to the Boy's Room (our bedroom) to get clean clothes on, wash up and patch up in the bathroom and get ready for a "little trip." We dabbed blood and sweat off each other's face and knuckles and actually giggled softly about how much fun that three block fist fight was. We were warriors. We looked like warriors. We fought like warriors, and we weren't only proud of ourselves––we were proud of each other! It was a *Battle Royale.*

"Okay, boys––downstairs and get in the car!" Dad was in a real serious mood. We got in the car and hoped we weren't going to Boys Town. Mom finally spoke, "I called Father Peckus. He is waiting for you two in the confessional."

Oh, dear God, we liked Father Peckus, but when he got mad, he got mean. Confession to Father Peckus for a measly little three block fist fight? It didn't seem fair!

When we got out of the car, Mom and Dad drove away. We shuffled into church and there stood Father Peckus, by the confessional. He shot us a mean look and stepped into *"THE BOX."*

Who would go first? It was Snap, and I admired his courage. He entered "the box," and I could hear Father Peckus growling. A minute later Snap walked out, knelt down beside me and didn't look up.

My turn. I went in and started my required opening remarks. "Bless me Father, for I have sinned ..." but before I could say anymore, he asked, "What's the matter with you two? Are you stupid or something?"

I was about to say, "Yes," but then he told me if this ever happens again, he's going to use more than words. I knew he had a big wooden paddle and I'm sure that's what he was talking about. Then he said, "Now, you and your brother go home and say a rosary and say it together. Do you hear me?"

I said, "Yes, Father."

Then he said, "Go on, get out of here. Go home."

Still can't figure out why he was in such a bad mood.

We jogged out of church and when we got a block away we started laughing. I don't know why we started laughing. It must have been because we were "stupid." We were straight-faced by the time we got home and, when we walked in the house, Mom and Dad didn't say anything. I asked them if it was okay if we went to our fort in the jungle and Mom said, "Okay, but we are going to eat in a half hour."

We ran out into the jungle and climbed up into the second floor of our fort. We talked about saying the rosary and decided we'd better do it. We didn't have a rosary in the fort. We just had a little silver cross we kept there because we really did like Jesus and we knew that, most of the time, he liked us, too. So we decided to use our fingers and we were praying in a whisper when, all of a sudden, there was a knock on the roof of the fort.

It was Dad. He asked, "Are you boys in there?"

"Yes."

"Your mother and I have been thinking about you and we think it's important that you know something."

Snap said, "Okay."

Then Dad said, "Your Mom is here and she wants to say it."

We were both pretty nervous by now because that "Boys Town" thing kept going through our minds.

"Boys, your father and I want you to know that, even though sometimes you are bad and make us worry, we still love you very much. Having you two in our lives keeps us from ever having a dull day."

We weren't sure what she meant by that, but we did know that, for some reason, Mom and Dad were being nice. Then Mom said, "Did you hear what I said?"

We both said, "Yes."

"You are good boys and we want you to know we love you."

We said, "Okay."

Now Dad took his turn and said, "Are you boys okay in there?"

"Yes."

"What are you doing?"

This time we had to tell the whole truth, but before we did we had a few questions they had to answer first.

"If we tell you what we're doing, do you promise not to laugh?"

"Yes."

"Do you promise to believe us?"

"Of course, we will."

"Do you promise not to tell anyone?"

"Boys, we won't tell anyone. Now what are you doing in there that's such a big secret?"

"Okay, don't laugh. We're in here ...

"PRAYING THE ROSARY!"

Chapter 23

GHOST IN THE ATTIC

"The Door Just Opened!"

Dateline: 1955 – Ages 11 & 10

Our little brother, Barry, was born in 1950. He was a fine little fella and we loved him a lot; and to show our love, we gave him a lot of attention by teasing him a lot. There was never any harm intended. He was good-natured and believed almost everything we told him. When he was three, we nicknamed him "Toad" and he liked it. Everyone called him Toad, except Mom and Dad.

One of the ways we lovingly teased Toad was to scare him. Some of the scary stories we told him he'd want us to "prove it," so we'd just drop it. But there was one scary story we thought we'd have some fun with. It was Christmas time and we told Toad that *Marley's Ghost* lived in our attic. He just told us to, "Shut up!" and, "There's no such thing as ghosts, because Mom and Dad said so." We told him that not even Mom and

Dad knew that *Marley's Ghost* lived in our attic, but me and Snap did because we went up there and we saw him.

Toad said we were liars and threatened to tell Mom and Dad we were trying to scare him. That's one thing about Toad––he was always squealing on us and getting us in trouble.

But this time, we told him we would show him *Marley's Ghost* if he promised not to tell Mom and Dad. As I recall, we offered him twenty-five cents, some candy, and a "nice" ghost.

He agreed!

It was about 8:00 in the evening and we took him into our sister Judy's room. There were two single beds in there. Snap got into one and Toad and I got into the other. There was a linen closet in the room, so me and Snap had opened it slightly, tied some string around the door handle, and ran the string up to the bed that Toad and I were in. Toad didn't see the string.

We told Toad that sometimes *Marley's Ghost* came down out of the attic into the house and that he always came down through that linen closet. Once again, he called us liars.

Snap began to pound on the wall and claim it was old, dead *Marley* roaming around in the attic looking for the door to come down into our room. Toad told us he was getting scared and that we should stop. We assured him that he was safe with us, but scared or not, *Marley* was on his way down.

Toad pulled the covers up to his neck and I gently pulled the string on the door. Snap said, "Here he comes!" and the door just opened.

Toad went ballistic.

He dove under the covers and screamed like a banshee. We knew Mom and Dad had to have heard that blood-curdling scream. We tried to calm him down by telling him it was a joke and that we were just teasing him. We showed him the string and offered him the candy and money, but he was freaking out and we knew what was going to hit the fan ... **AND IT DID!**

Mom came storming into the room; it was very apparent she was on a mission. As soon as Toad saw her, he rushed into her arms. Boy, was she upset! We had never seen her that mad before. As a matter of fact, if she wasn't a pacifist, I'm sure she would have knocked us both ass-over-appetite!

She demanded to know what happened. Toad started telling her about *Marley's Ghost* and the door and all that stuff. We knew our goose was cooked. The infamous event closed with the following conversation:

"Look at your little brother––he's shaking. Did you think you were being funny by scaring the daylights out of him?"

"Yes."

"Do you realize now that this isn't funny? That it's harmful?"

"Yes."

"Do you realize you should tell Barry you're sorry?"

"Yes."

"Is that all you can do is stand there and say yes?"

"Yes."

"You two are really getting on my nerves. If either one of you say "yes" one more time I'm going to slap both of you. Do you hear me?"

"No." (A tiny little smile crossed her face.)

"Are you two sick or what?"

"No."

"Sometimes I think you both need professional help."

"What's professional help?"

"Professional help is when a different kind of doctor tries to fix what's wrong with different kinds of people--**LIKE YOU TWO**!"

"Now, go to bed and don't you ever, ever scare your little brother ever again! Understand?"

"No."

With that, she hugged Toad, took him out of the room, shot us another angry look, and slammed the door. Snap looked at me and said, "John, how do you feel?"

More of and the Best of Me & Snap

"I feel pretty good. How do you feel?"

Snap said, "I feel really good too ...

"WONDER WHY SHE THINKS WE'RE SICK?"

Chapter 24

PEASHOOTERS

Band Day

Dateline: Fall, 1954 – Ages 9 & 10

Every kid in Carroll owned a peashooter back in those days. You could buy them at Nolands, Lee's, or Woolworths for only a dime. They looked like big, fat straws. Each one was about ten inches long, with an opening on both ends the size of a nickel. The ammunition for these less-than-lethal weapons was white navy beans. For another dime, you could buy a big sack of them at Fareway. Mr. Singsang, the manager of Fareway, always smiled when he saw us little guys buying navy beans. He knew what was going on!

It was a chilly, Saturday, October morning. Me and Snap were in the back yard shooting hoops, when we heard a loud racket in the front yard. We checked it out and found band kids lining up in the street, blowing on their horns and pounding on their drums. It was Band Day in Carroll. We stood around and watched them for a little bit. They were nice kids. They smiled at us and said, "Hi," and we returned their greeting.

I don't know what possessed us, but we went in the house, got our peashooters, filled our mouths with navy beans, and re-joined the band kids.

Moving within about ten feet of them, we opened fire!

We must have blown 50-60 beans at them and, as they were zinging off their horns and trumpets, they made a funny kind of music. The band kids apparently didn't like our kind of music, though, because five or six of them put their instruments down on the grass and came after us.

They were high school kids, but couldn't catch us. It was no contest. They had on big wool uniforms, heavy boots, and tall hats. We were in jeans, sweatshirts, and P.F. Flyers (cool tennis shoes). We ran through our back yard, up the hill, into the jungle, and up into the safety of our tree fort. When we looked out of the fort, we saw them walking back to the street. It wasn't even close––another "W" for me and Snap!

However, the victory celebration didn't last long. Mom came out the back door and was marching towards the jungle. Oh, crap! We hunkered down, so she couldn't see us. When she arrived at the foot of the tree, she barked out an angry question.

"Are you two up there?"

We were thinking about saying no, but figured she wouldn't believe us, so answered ...

"Yes."

"Get down here! Right now! Both of you!"

We hustled down and stood side-by-side with hands in our pockets. We were in deep, deep trouble again.

"Give me those peashooters!"

We handed them over, and she began to twist and bend them. She was really mad. But, you know what? Those peashooters were indestructible! No matter what she did, they just popped back to their original form! Her face was getting red.

"Mom, they won't break."

"Be quiet!"

She finally gave up and put them in the pocket of her apron.

"I don't know, boys. I've tried everything with you two. I take your allowance away, that doesn't work. I ground you, that doesn't work. I take away movies and roller skating and that doesn't work. I spank you, that doesn't work. I'm not sure what's next."

She was really, really mad, so we tried to appeal to the soft part of her heart.

"Mom, please don't think about adopting us out to another family. We like it here. It's really fun."

"Adopt you out? I never thought of that before, but it's a good idea."

When she said, "It's a good idea," we all started laughing really hard. Mom was laughing so hard she was holding her stomach. When she finally stopped she looked right at us and said, "You two get your skinny little butts up in that tree nest or tree house or whatever you call it and stay there until I tell you to come down."

"It's a tree fort."

"I don't care! Get up there."

We hustled up there and when we got in she said, "Now, stay there!" then started walking toward the house.

"How long do you think we will be here?"

"I'm not sure––two or three days."

"Two or three days? We could starve to death!"

"HO! HO! HO!"

"It's not funny, Mom. We are already getting hungry and we look really skinny."

"That's too bad."

"Mom, we're sorry."

"No, you're not."

"YES, WE ARE!"

She didn't stop. She just kept walking to the house.

"Hey, Mom, WE LOVE YOU!"

That stopped her, but she didn't turn around. She put her arms straight up in the air and looked up at the sky. She stayed like that for a minute or two. It kind of worried us. We thought maybe she had one of those strokes, where your body becomes frozen, but she didn't tip over, so we figured it wasn't one of those things. Then our little brains figured out what she was really doing. She was ...

TALKING TO GOD ABOUT US!

Chapter 25

KILLED A COW

"What's a Bazooka?"

Dateline: Summer 1950-1958 – Ages 6 to 13

We loved going to the creek. It was one of our favorite places to hang out when we weren't doing all that other stuff. The creek was east of our house, through the Jungle and about three city blocks across cornfields and pastureland. We'd take our BB guns, Boy Scout hatchets, some snackin' stuff and best friend––our dog, Fritz. Fritzy was a ten-pound, toy Manchester who went with us everywhere. We loved that little mutt!

We always had a lot of fun at the creek. There were frogs and turtles and water bugs and grasshoppers and snakes and horses and cows and even a donkey. One very mean-spirited donkey!

As we got about three hundred yards from the big pool part of the creek there was very tall, thick grass, that today is called switch grass. But we kids called it elephant grass and this elephant grass had a three-foot-wide path, all the way from start to finish. The path was the handiwork of that mean donkey. Now, when we were going to and from the creek, it was a lot easier for us to walk down that donkey trail than it was to push our way through that elephant grass, but whenever that donkey heard us coming, it would lay its ears back and come thundering down the path with bad intentions.

Well, the donkey never did get us because it wouldn't ever veer off that path into the elephant grass. So, when it got close, all we did was take a few steps back into the elephant grass and that old donkey would go roaring right past us. Now remember, we didn't start the bad feelings between us and that donkey. The donkey started it! So, occasionally when he would run past us, we would step out behind him and pepper his big fat butt with some well-aimed BB pellets. Boy, would he get mad and make some angry noises!

We used to like to hang around the deep part of the creek. We'd catch frogs and turtles and shoot water bugs and, for many years, unsuccessfully tried to kill a poisonous water moccasin. That ugly old snake sent us packin' many times. We would see him floating on a branch or a log and we'd open fire. He'd get alarmed and slither into the water in our direction and we'd head for the Jungle.

One day when Snap and I were out there shooting water bugs, Police Chief Bruening pulled up on the road right next to the creek and said, "Boys, come over here."

Oh, my God, it wasn't just the cops, it was the Chief. Dad told us he was a good man and ran a good police department, but we never thought the day would come that his job would have anything to do with us.

Well, that day did come and we weren't sure if we were going to poop our pants or head for the Jungle. Before either one of those things occurred he said, "You are not in trouble; I just want to talk to you."

We looked at each other, laid our BB guns down in the grass, and started walking toward this cop. He stopped us and said, "Bring your BB guns with you; that's what I want to talk to you about."

Oh man, we were scared. Someone probably reported us for accidentally shooting out their window, or accidentally shooting out a street light, or accidentally shooting a robin, or maybe even accidentally blasting that old donkey in the butt. Whatever, we figured he was tricking us and was going to haul us off to jail. When we got a few steps from this black and white police car he said, "Get in!"

He ordered both of us to get in the front seat and we did. We knew Mom and Dad were really going to be mad at us when we called to tell them we were in jail. Chief Bruening started his cop car and said, "Boys, did you know you were shooting your BB guns within the city limits?"

The city limits? We were at the creek. Downtown Carroll was a mile away so we said, "No."

Then he said, "You were shooting your BB guns on that side of the road and that's within city limits. That means you were breaking the law."

Snap immediately said, "If you don't put us in jail, we promise to never shoot our BB guns ever again." Back then (we were only seven and eight), we'd say anything to stay out of jail.

"Boys, you are not going to jail. I'm just going to drive you around Carroll and show you the city limits so you know where you can and cannot shoot your guns."

Fair enough, but we didn't want anyone seeing us in the cop car so we slid down and peeked over the dash. That ride around Carroll lasted about a month, but when he dropped us off back at the creek he said, "Boys, that only took a half an hour, but I want you to remember what you learned today."

"We will."

He smiled and drove off. Me and Snap dodged another bullet!

One other day after school, we were at the creek messin' around, just Snap, Cy Farner and me. We were just doing our thing, blasting water bugs and talking about our teachers. As we were carrying on, we noticed a bunch of big, black cows moving toward us. We always liked those cows. We pretended they were buffaloes. I don't know what it was they were interested in that day, but they kept getting closer and closer. They were starting to scare us a little bit, so we picked up dirt clods and started throwing them. One of those big black cows got about six feet from us and someone launched a dirt clod that smacked it right between the eyes. That old cow's two front legs buckled and it crashed to the ground. **Oh, my God, we killed a cow!**

We ran all the way home, each guy denying he threw the fatal dirt clod. Before we went into the house we reminded each other of the "Code of Silence."

At supper that night Dad asked us how our day went. We said school was good and that we went to the creek.

He asked, "What did you do at the creek?"

We said, "Aw, just shot water bugs and messed around."

Then he said, "It's a good thing you guys have BB guns and not bazookas."

We asked him what a bazooka was and he said, "It's a big gun they used in World War II. It shot bullets so big it could ...

"KILL A COW!"

("Oh, Crap!")

Chapter 26

POOPED MY PANTS

"Buried in the Jungle"

Dateline: 1953 – Ages 9 & 8

One late afternoon in the early fall of 1953, Snap, CY and I were in the Jungle just kinda hanging out and looking for a little action. We knew that someone was building a big new house on the northeast corner of "our" Jungle, so we decided to scout it out. When we got there, we huddled behind a huge pile of dirt about 30 feet from the new structure. The walls were up. The roof was on. And the contractor and owners of the house were in there, walking around and talking about stuff we really didn't understand.

You know by now that we were little guys who imagined ourselves as warriors, cowboys, supermen and soldiers. So at this particular time, one of us suggested that we lob some hand grenades on the roof of this new house to disrupt all the fun they seemed to be having.

All three of us thought that was a great idea, so we all grabbed a big dirt clod, kept our elbows locked, (as WWII army guys did) and launched our dirt clod hand grenades onto the roof.

BOOM, BOOM, BOOM!

All three were direct hits on the roof––right above where they were standing. We heard them shout, "What in the heck was that?"

One of the men said, "I think I know."

This was way too much fun. Those people didn't have a clue. I said to Snap and CY, "Reload!"

We each grabbed another hand grenade, locked our elbows, and launched. Direct hits––BOOM, BOOM, BOOM!

Didn't get much more fun than that––until all of a sudden out of nowhere––this humongous adult man jumps out at us and screams, "What the hell are you kids doing?"

Total shock. My entire mind, body and soul were devastated. Nothing like this had ever happened to me before. When he appeared out of nowhere and hollered, "What the hell are you kids doing?" I POOPED MY PANTS!

God's truth. I couldn't believe it. I was on my knees when it happened and I had no idea what to do. I froze. This man kept hollering at us and telling us we were good kids, so he couldn't understand why we were behaving like this. He went on and on.

I was so unprepared for all of this, I just started nervously laughing. I couldn't stop. Snap and Cy started laughing, and the more we laughed, the angrier our new neighbor got. Finally, after chewing our butts out for a good ten minutes, he said, "Now get the hell out of here before I really get mad!"

Heck, we had the impression he already was really mad, but we did as he ordered and retreated deep into the Jungle. When we got there, I told Snap and Cy that this guy's sudden appearance and loud hollering shocked my system so severely that, "I pooped my pants!"

Oh man, did they laugh! And that was okay, but when they finally got over it, I made them promise they would never, never, ever tell anyone that I pooped my pants. They said they would never tell. They were my best friends, and I knew I could trust them.

A couple of problems still remained. I needed some clean jeans and skivvies. I asked Snap to sneak in the house and round up some clean clothes for me. While he was gone, I went into our Jungle fort, took off my soiled clothes, and used the toilet paper there to clean up as best I could. In a few minutes, Snap was back. I put on the clean skivs and jeans. Then we discussed the one final problem. What should we do with the dirty clothes?

I couldn't tell Mom and Dad that I pooped my pants. I was nine years old. **Nine-year-olds don't poop their pants!** If I did admit to pooping my pants, they would start asking a bunch of questions. I didn't want to tell them that we had launched an unprovoked attack against our new neighbors in their new house, and when he counter attacked I ... well––lost it!

There was only one thing we could do––get rid of the evidence. Hide 'em. Burn 'em. Bury 'em. Bury 'em in the Jungle. Once again, Snap was called upon to go home undetected, get Dad's spade and return to the Jungle.

He did a great job. We dug a two-foot hole, buried the evidence and got home just in time for supper. Only one problem. Dad and Mom saw us put the spade back in the garage.

Well, we sat down for supper, prayed and filled our plates; then, the dreaded conversation began.

Mom very pointedly asked, "Boys, what were you doing with the spade? Snap, I saw you carrying it, so what did you guys use it for? Now tell me the truth, I don't want any more of your buried treasure or other funny stories."

"Okay, Mom. We were playing in the Jungle. John accidentally pooped his pants. He didn't want you to know, so we buried his jeans in the Jungle."

Snap always had a way of making Mom and Dad laugh, so when he told them this, they cracked up.

When they composed themselves, Mom said...

"VERY FUNNY, SNAP. NOW, WHAT REALLY HAPPENED?"

Chapter 27

ELEVATOR

Dateline: Fall 1958

I was a freshman at Kuemper Catholic High School in Carroll. It was a great school and I loved being a big high school kid.

The freshmen had their classes in the old wing of the school, up on the 3rd floor. The rooms seemed big and dark and kinda cold, but it didn't matter––we were a pretty happy bunch. The one intriguing thing about the 3rd floor freshmen hall was that there was an old elevator there and it still worked––well, kinda worked. The only ones allowed to use it were teachers and kids with disabilities. If anyone else got caught using it, they would be sent down to visit with the Principal, Father Tom Donahoe. Father Donahoe was a great guy and a really good coach and we all liked him, but he was the Principal and you didn't want to be sent to the Principal's Office.

Well, I have to admit, some of us guys rode that old elevator a couple of times, but we never did get caught. We did, however, get in trouble because of that elevator. You see, when we were riding that noisy old monster, we discovered something goofy about it. When it got up to the third floor, if someone outside the elevator pushed the "down button," it would slam the door and drop all the way to first floor. Anyway, no one in the elevator could stop it from doing that. It had a mind of its own––or a screwy connection––one or the other, but that's the way it worked. We thought that was pretty cool, but one day all that changed.

It was the noon hour, we had just finished eating, and were wrestling around in the hallway by the elevator. We saw the elevator light go on and we had a pretty good idea what teacher was on board. It was Mr. K. Now, that's not his real name. I changed it to protect his privacy for very obvious reasons.

So, there we were, Mike Otto, Butch Conley, Steve Collison, Herby Dion and me, standing in front of the elevator. We liked Mr. K. To our delight, he would spend a part of each class period telling us about his school days, and especially, his college days. According to him, he was a pretty good athlete, and to prove it he would occasionally wear his college letter sweater to class. That was cool. There was one thing about Mr. K though, he had a short fuse and if he got mad––Katie, bar the door!

Well, back to the elevator. As it was about to reach the third floor, Otto stepped over by the button, and there was no doubt what that idiot was going to do. The elevator door opened just far enough for Mr. K to see our smiling faces when Otto hit the button. The door slammed, and down it went with Mr. K screaming our names all the way to the bottom!

We were terrified and speechless, but Mike just stood there smiling. Mr. K couldn't see him because he was pressed up against the wall by the button. As the elevator was coming back up, Mr. K was hollering,

"DON'T MOVE! DON'T MOVE, ANY OF YOU!"

We didn't move. Otto didn't move, either. We were trying not to smile as the elevator door began to open. But, guess what? Yep, the elevator door banged closed and down he went again––and was he ever making a racket!

Talk about scared! We knew it couldn't get much worse. We told Otto if he did it again we'd pound him. He stepped away from the button and off the elevator jumped Mr. K. His face was red and he was showing his teeth––two bad signs for us bad guys!

"Who was pushing the button?"

We all pointed to Mike.

"The rest of you guys thought that was pretty funny, didn't you?"

We all shook our heads, "No."

"Then why were you smiling and laughing?"

We just looked down at the floor.

"I can assure you of one thing, it will never happen again! Now, stand side-by-side and put your hands down to your sides. NOW!"

We knew what was going to happen. We'd been slapped and spanked before, so we were ready. IT WAS SHOW TIME! At least 50 or 60 of our classmates were watching the drama unfold. He stared at us as he moved back and forth in front of us. First to his left, then to his right, then back again. He stopped, loaded up his right slapping hand and moved in for the execution. He whacked each of us alongside the head. POP, POP, POP, POP, POP. He was really strong. When he popped me, it felt like my head spun around three or four times, and when it stopped spinning my eyeballs were crooked. That's the truth!

Then he got in our faces again.

"Now, how funny was that, boys?"

"It wasn't funny."

"Not funny, sir."

"Not funny."

"Not funny, Mr. K."

"Sorry, Sir."

"I'm not finished with you. For the next week, every day at 12:25, I want all of you to be standing right here facing the elevator. I will be getting off at that time and I'll be looking right at each one of you, and I better not see the slightest smile or grin. Do you understand me?"

We all nodded our heads and said, "Yes."

Now remember, there were a lot of kids who had just heard and witnessed what happened. As it turned out, that was not good.

We gathered in front of that old elevator for the next three school days and greeted Mr. K with a straight face. Everything was fine until the fourth day. We were lined up, straight-faced as the elevator was approaching the 3rd floor at 12:25. As you might expect, there was an audience every day, and until this day, everyone was well-behaved. But suddenly, out of the audience, stepped our good buddy, Frog Reinhart. He moved quickly to the elevator button. We were horrified. We hollered ...

"FROG! NOOOO!"

About that time, the elevator door started to open ...

"OH, CRAP!"

Chapter 28

CONTRAPTIONS

"The Dawn of NASCAR"

Dateline: Early-Middle 1950s

Contraptions? Yep, that's what they were and we assembled them. We were not skilled craftsmen, automakers, designers, or anything like that. But, we did slap together some four-wheel pieces of junk, and recklessly rode them down *The Ferlic Hill*.

The Ferlic Hill, three blocks west of our house, was so-named by us because Doctor Ferlic and his good family lived in a beautiful home halfway down the north side of that steep incline.

We scraped up wagon wheels, buggy wheels, two-by-fours, four-by-fours, plywood, and old throw rugs and nailed all the pieces together. They became our "Go Carts," "Soap Box Carts," and "Kamikaze Carts." They were all just a bunch of contraptions and we rode them hard and we rode them often.

They were dangerous.

They were deadly.

They were fun.

And God only knows how we lived through those races.

Did we have any kind of crash helmets? Are you kidding? The only crash helmets we had was the hair on our heads!

Did we have seats and seatbelts? Are you kidding? Our seats were our backs, bellies and butts! The only belts we had were the ones that held our jeans up.

We rode those suicide machines down the hill several ways – sitting on our butts, laying on our backs, or lying face down on our bellies. The "belly ride" was the most popular, because it was easier to bail out just before the CRASH!

What sort of steering wheel or turning mechanism did we have? Are you kidding? We didn't know how to make those things turn! We'd just pull them up the hill, aim them where we wanted to go, jump on, fly down that hill, and pray that our Guardian Angel was on board.

Did we have brakes? Are you kidding? The only brakes we had were trees, bushes, houses, parked cars and an occasional light post! Did we ever get hurt? Does an elephant poop in the jungle?

So, why did we do that crazy stuff?

Why did we put ourselves in harm's way?

Well, near as I can tell, we did it because it was fun and because we were 50's kids. Also, because we were youthful, adventuresome, and fearless. But mostly, we did it because ... WE WERE STUPID!

As a matter of fact, I remember one time when a bunch of us guys were flying down that hill. There must have been 10 to 12 of us. I'm not exactly sure who was there, but there were a lot of guys who lived close by – Me and Snap, Cy and Steve Farner, Bob Pudenz, Tom Feld, Mike and Larry Otto, Fred Ferlic, Bob Benholtz, Tim White, Mike Wittrock, Jimmy Wilson, Brian Fitzpatrick, Ray Beck, Pat Moehn, Dick Gnam, Terry Hyland, Terry Frank, Butch Thomas, Tom and Fred Dolezal, the Crouse boys, the Martin boys, Frog Reinhart, the Kelly boys, the Stone boys, and the Murphy boys – just to mention a few. Anyway, we always had a spotter at the bottom of the hill, watching for cars, because we zoomed down and right across a very busy North West Street. Terry Frank's driveway, across that busy street, was our target. We didn't hit the target very often, but that's where we were aiming most of the time.

On this particular day, at this particular time, I was the spotter. I couldn't see any cars coming from any direction, so I dropped my arm. That was the "All Clear" signal. Down the hill came a "double" – two guys riding on one contraption. I think it was Pudy (Bob Pudenz) and Big Red (Mike Otto). They were *hell bent for election,* but as they got about halfway down the hill, a car came speeding up from the south.

Oh boy, it was going to be close! I was waving at Big Red and Pudy, but they didn't see me because they were just *hangin' on for dear life!* No one was going to stop. Just as those two kamikazes started across North West Street, the car slammed on its brakes. I'm happy to report that Pudy and Big Red landed safely in Frank's driveway. It wasn't even close. That car missed them by a good twenty feet.

The driver wasn't very happy, though! He was an older fella, about forty. Jumping out of the car in a fit of road rage, the guy started yelling and swearing at us. "You little a**holes! What the hell are you doing? I just about killed those two idiots! Are you STUPID or what?"

Well, that was a "no brainer." We all knew we were stupid. No one ever stopped and asked, "Are you smart or what?"

He chewed us out for a little while longer, then said, "Now, get the hell out of here! Go home! I know all your parents and if I ever see you here again, I'm going to call them AND the cops!" You know, when I think about it, there were some adults in the 50's, who just ... didn't have a sense of humor!

Then, he got into his car and peeled out. When he was out of sight, I gave the "All Clear" signal – and down the hill came three more contraptions ...

HELL BENT FOR ELECTION!

Chapter 29

SNAP'S BEEN KIDNAPPED

"I Know Where He Is!"

Dateline: March 15, 1950 – Age: Snap was 4

In Carroll, Iowa in 1950 there wasn't a lot of excitement. Oh, occasionally a car would smash a dog and all the kids would run out in the street to look at the guts and blood. And, once in awhile, some idiot would shoot out a street light and the neighbors would call the cops, but other than that, it was a peaceful, quiet little town. No murders, no kidnappings, no bar room brawls, no bank robberies, no nothing––until March 15, 1950, when the APB came across the police radio: *"Robert Brian Bruner, age 4, has been kidnapped."*

We were little guys, but we knew our way around the neighborhood. There was no way we could get lost within our playground, which was a six-square-block area. There were no bad people who lived there and there were no bad guys that would dare come there, but on this day, something goofy was going on. Snap was attending preschool at Mrs. Winniky's on this morning and for some reason I was home. Mrs. Winniky's was only three blocks from our house, so when the weather was okay, we'd walk there and walk home.

Well, the weather was good this day and at 11:15 a.m. preschool was out, so Snap headed for home. All the kids in the neighborhood were friends and Snap bumped into a couple of them on the way home. He and Butch Thomas built a few little mud forts in the street and then he pushed on to Ray Beck's house. Ray was five years old and for some reason was home alone for a little while. Ray had a neat basement in his house and we liked hanging out down there. It was like a cave. Like a fort. Anyway, Snap and Ray got to having fun and time just sorta slipped away.

Snap should have been home by 11:30 and it was noon. Mom had lunch ready and she was worried. She called Mrs. Winniky and was told Snap left with the rest of the kids at 11:15. Mom called the Kellys, the Martins, the Dolezals, the Farners, the Becks, the Wilsons, the Pudenzes, the Moens, the Stones, the Pringels, the Millers, the Schaefers, the Mormons, the Thomases, the Annebergs, and the Fitzpatricks. NO SNAP.

Mom called Dad who came rushing home. It was 12:15 p.m. and still no Snap. Mom called the nuns and Dad called the cops. By 12:30, we had cops and nuns in the house and neighbors all over the place. Mom was praying with the nuns and dad was talking to the cops. I couldn't understand what all the fuss was about. Snap was probably at Ray Beck's house.

I told Mom I'd go get him and she said, "Oh, no you won't! You aren't leaving the yard. I don't want to lose you, too!"

I went up to Dad and told him and a couple of cops that Snap was at Ray Beck's house and he told me the police already checked that out and he wasn't there.

"If Snap sees the cops, he will hide from them. I know where he's hiding."

"John, we are going to let the police handle this. That is their job."

I still couldn't believe what a big deal everyone was making of this. It's now 1:00 and there must have been a hundred people standing around our front yard. Three or four of those little Ford black and white cop cars were parked out in front and a dozen nuns and priests were continuing to pray with Mom in the living room. Everyone was beginning to think that poor little Snap was a goner. Only a miracle could bring him back.

Now, Snap knew something wasn't quite right and when the cops showed up at Ray Beck's house, he hid behind a chair and Ray told the police, "Snap's not here. It's only me."

When the cops left, Ray and Snap went down to the basement to play. Ray's dad came home about 1:15 and gruffly told Snap, "Get home, everyone is looking for you!"

Snap slipped out the back door and headed home. He crouched low, staying behind trees and bushes, and actually got within thirty feet of our house, totally undetected, until Mom saw him and screamed, "**There he is!**"

With that loud proclamation, Snap stood up straight and stepped out from behind the bushes. And there, for one brief shining moment, stood Robert Brian Bruner—four-foot-two, red cowboy hat, black and brown cowboy boots, dusty old blue jeans and twin six-shooters, strapped low and ready to go.

The whole world took a deep, collective breath and with grateful eyes consumed the miracle of his presence, which was nothing less than ...

MAGNIFICENT!

Chapter 30

BATTLESHIP TITANIC

"Lost at Sea"

Dateline: Summer 1957 – Ages 13 & 12

We hopped on our bikes and headed for Swan Lake with our Boy Scout hatchets and a couple bags of long nails, shoe laces, and leather strips. *Swan Pond*, as we called it, was a State Park three miles south of Carroll, with a 200-300 acre lake and lots of trees. We had a plan, and now it was time to do it.

We rode our bikes around to the south central part of the lake where there was a sandy beach and lots of trees. We parked them close to water and set about our business. We were going to build a raft and sail it across *Swan Pond* to a part of the lake that had never been explored. The northwest corner of Swan Lake, as legend had it, was inhabited by bandits, bad guys, escaped convicts, and wild animals. We really, really needed to go there because we really, really needed to discover the truth for ourselves.

We chopped down at least a dozen small trees, stripped the branches off, chopped the trunks into five - foot logs, nailed two levels together, and secured the nailed logs with shoe laces and leather strips. It was ready––our pride and joy. The raft was solid and going to take us to the North Shore. She was beautiful and we named her the *TITANIC*.

It was a hot, humid, dry, drought summer day so we took off our T-shirts, kicked off our tennis shoes, rolled up our jeans, and boarded the *TITANIC*. We each had a seven-foot-long pole that we carved out of a couple of tall skinny trees. These would serve as our oars and rudder, and we knew how to use them. We launched the *TITANIC* from the same sandy beach on which we built her. She floated and we were standing on her, headed towards the legendary North Shore.

It was exciting because this homemade ship was really floating and we were a couple of proud little dudes. We were out there two hundred yards, and then another two hundred yards, and we were going to land on the North Shore. Well, we weren't really going to "land." We were going to "look," then get out of there as fast as we could. Deep down, we were scared of what we were about to see.

Well, as luck would have it, we didn't get a chance to either "look" or "land." Water was pouring through the bottom of the *TITANIC*. It was above our ankles. It wasn't sinking––it was separating! It was floating apart. The nails, the shoe laces, the leather strips——they didn't hold. We were in the water and swimming as frantically as we could for the South Shore. We swam sixty or seventy yards and were out of gas in the middle of Swan Lake. Snap said, "John, can you help me? I'm going down."

I said, "I'll try," but as I put my arm around his shoulder, we both went down, feet first——down, down, down, to the muddy old bottom of Swan Pond.

But something happened on the way to our drowning. Our feet were on the bottom, but our heads were above the water. The drought was so bad and the lake was so low, we were actually touching. We could walk on the bottom! It was gooey mud and gooey silt, but we could walk and we could breath and we weren't dead. Praise God, we'd dodged another bullet!

It took us fifteen minutes to walk out of that hell hole and when we got out, we laid on that sandy beach for a half an hour. We were spent. Once our skinny little bodies recovered a measure of energy, we climbed on our bikes and peddled the three miles home. We were dirty and we were stinky and when Mom saw us she asked, "For gosh sakes, where have you boys been?"

We told her, "Swan Pond," and she asked us what we were doing there. We told her we built a raft and named it the *TITANIC*. Mom said, "You boys didn't cut down trees at Swan Lake?"

We told her we did and she informed us it was a crime to cut down trees in a state park. Heck, that was news to us. We'd been cutting trees down at *Swan Pond* for a long time.

Mom looked kinda worried, and then she asked why we named our raft the *TITANIC*. We told her it was the only name of a battleship that we knew, so we used it. Then she dropped a bomb and told us, "Boys, the *TITANIC* was not a battleship; it was a big passenger ship and it sunk to the bottom of the ocean on its maiden voyage."

We asked her what a "maiden voyage" was and she explained that it was the "first trip it made." Wow, just like our *TITANIC*, except ours didn't sink. It just floated all over the lake.

Mom asked what we did with the raft and we told her we put it in the water and rode around on it for awhile. Mom said, "Boys, that's a dangerous, old dirty lake. If that raft didn't hold you, you could have drowned! And, by the way, you guys don't know how to build a raft––did someone help you?"

Snap said, "No, we were the only ones at the lake."

Mom asked, "What did you do with this raft when you were done riding it?"

I said, "We rode it out to the middle of Swan Pond, it broke all apart and floated all over the lake. Me and Snap were drowning, but the lake is so low now we were able to touch the bottom, so we walked to shore."

Mom just stared at us and then said, "You two are muddy and stinky. Go to the basement shower."

We started down the basement steps and Mom said, "Boys, stop! I just have to know one thing and I want you to tell me the absolute truth. All that raft stuff really didn't happen, did it?"

"NO, MOM!"

Chapter 31

GOLFING BLACK BIRDS

"What's So Funny?"

Dateline: 1954 – Ages 10 & 9

One day in June or July of 1954, Mom called Snap and me into the kitchen and said, "Boys, those black birds are eating so many of those cherries in our tree, I don't think there will be any left for me to make pies or jam. I'm just sick about it. I need you two to help me keep those birds out of our cherry tree."

Snap asked, "Do you want us to shoot 'em?"

"Oh, I don't know, but you have got to help me."

I said, "Mom, the only way to get them out of there is to shoot 'em!"

"Okay, do what you have to, but don't tell your dad I gave you permission to shoot them with your BB guns. Promise?"

"We promise. But Mom, when we shoot them, what do you want us to do with them?"

She responded, "What did you do with all the other birds you've shot? I haven't seen any of them lying around the neighborhood, and I know you are shooting them because we don't hear birds singing around here in the morning."

That was a cheap shot (pardon the pun)! Every kid on the block had a BB gun. We didn't shoot all those early morning song birds. Heck, we were still sleeping when those birds started to make all that racket.

Anyway, we devised a plan. One of us would climb the tree with our BB gun, shoot those thievin' black birds, and the other guy would get rid of them.

You know, we were not very smart. We reasoned to ourselves that if they were not in our yard––no problem. So, we decided that the guy below the tree would simply put them in someone else's yard. But how would we do that?

Snap––genius that he was––came up with the perfect solution. "Let's use Uncle Cliff's golf club and just knock them over the hedge into Mr. Maher's backyard."

Perfect! I climbed the tree and Snap was on the ground with a vintage nine-iron from the 20's. The birds were all over the place, gobbling up Mom's pie and jam. I took careful aim and began dropping them on top of Snap. He carefully measured them, and then launched them over a five-foot high hedge into Mr. Maher's backyard. It wasn't necessarily a work of art, but it was working. We were just about to celebrate our victory over these berry-eating invaders when, from around the hedge, appeared Mr. Maher holding two or three birds in each hand. I jumped out of the tree and he stomped up to within five feet of us asking, "Are these your birds?"

Let me tell you, Mr. Maher was a good man and we liked him, but at this moment we were scared spitless——or something like that. Snap, never one to tell a lie when caught in the act, answered, "Yes."

Then Mr. Maher said, "If these are your birds, what the **HELL** are they doing in **my** backyard?"

I told him the story about cherry pies and jam and that Mom told us to get rid of the black birds. He stood there holding those birds and said, "Let me get this straight. These birds were eating all the cherries in this big tree, so your mom told you to shoot them. Is that right?"

"Yes sir," replied our spokesman, Snap.

"So, John climbed the tree and shot them?"

"Yes, sir."

"So when they fell to the ground, Snap threw them in my backyard?"

"No, sir."

"Then how the **HELL** did they get in my backyard?"

"I golfed them over there, Mr. Maher."

"You golfed them into my backyard?"

"Yes, sir, but from now on I'm going to golf them into the Jungle."

Mr. Maher pointed to the Jungle, then held the birds up a little higher, looked right at both of us and said, "You two are the most unbelievable little sh _ _ s that God ever created!"

Then he dropped the birds, turned, and walked away. We noticed as he walked toward his house that his shoulders were shaking. We knew that meant he was either laughing or crying. We sure hoped he wasn't crying; and, if he was laughing ...

WE COULDN'T FIGURE OUT WHAT WAS SO FUNNY!

Chapter 32

GOT IN TROUBLE

Dateline: October, 1958

High School was a blast! We met new friends, we had a different teacher for each subject, and we went to a different room for each class. That was cool stuff.

One of my new friends was a kid by the name of Butch Conley. We had fun all through high school and college and are still good buddies to this day. But here's a little background on Butch––he was a practical joker. All the nuns really liked him and believed everything he said ... CON ARTIST! Now remember, back in those days of Catholic school education, most of our teachers were nuns and we always addressed them as "Sister."

Let me tell you, on this day Conley really got the better of me. We were between classes and heading to history class. I loved history and always got good grades in that class. Our teacher was Sister Paulinda. She was a very little lady with a powerful personality and a mighty big presence in the classroom. I liked her, and I thought she like me, too.

Just as we were walking into her classroom, Butch stumbled and fumbled his way for 20-25 feet, dropped his books on the floor, and acted as if he about fell down. Then he turned and looked at me and said,

"Bruner, knock it off. I could have got hurt!"

Now listen, I did not trip him and everybody in that room knew it, except Sister Paulinda. I was looking right at Butch and laughing and he was trying his best not to burst out laughing himself. Sister came up to me and grabbed my ear and jerked it half way out of my head and said, "What's the matter with you? If George (his real name) would have fallen down, he could have been badly hurt!"

"Sister, I didn't trip him. He was faking it."

"You don't fake that kind of behavior. Now quit talking back to me and apologize to George."

"Sister, I didn't ..."

"Apologize! Right now!"

Well, old Butch did it to me again, and should have gotten an Oscar for Best Actor. Neither one of us could get the grin off our faces, but I did as I was told.

"I'm sorry for NOT tripping you."

"What did you say? Now say it right!"

"Butch, I'm sorry I tripped you."

"His name is not Butch, it's George. Now apologize to George!"

"GEORGE, I'm sorry I tripped you ... What's so funny? Look Sister, he's laughing!"

Actually, the whole class was laughing.

"Okay, both of you sit down and this better not ever happen again. Do you hear me?"

"Yes, Sister."

"I'm not talking to you, George. I'm talking to John."

"Yes, Sister."

She nailed me with a dirty look, then went to the front of the room.

"Okay, everybody, take everything off the top of your desk and I'll pass out the test. Remember, this test score will be half of your first quarter grade. Take your time and read the questions very carefully."

Oh, I forgot to mention, do you know where my desk was? Yep, I was sitting right behind GEORGE Conley.

I put my name on my answer sheet, read the first question and recorded my answer. Before I could even start reading the second question, Butch straightened up his back and started rolling his shoulders and arms back and forth and kept muttering.

"Knock it off, Bruner! Knock it off!"

Sister came barreling down the aisle and asked Butch, "What's going on here?"

"Bruner is trying to cheat off me. He keeps looking over my shoulder at my answer sheet."

Oh, good God, he just about won another Oscar––and again, at my expense. Sister grabbed my test with her left hand and my ear––same ear she grabbed before––with her right hand, and out into the hall we went. My ear has never been the same. Man, it hurt!

"John Bruner, I've had it with you."

"Sister, I wasn't cheating. Butch ... I mean George ... was just goofing around ..."

"QUIET! You stay out here until class is over. I'm going to call your parents. And, by the way, you got an 'F' on this test."

"Sister, please! I wasn't cheating. Don't call Mom and Dad! Pu-leeeez!"

"At the end of the school day, you come to my classroom."

"Sister, I have football practice at 3:30."

"I don't care. You are going to miss football today."

Crap, I just got an 'F' on a history test, my parents are coming to school, and now our football coach will kick my butt.

When my last class was finished at the end of the school day, I went straight to Sister's classroom. There she was and there was Mom and Dad. My stomach hurt, and I don't think I looked very good.

"Hi, John. How are you doing?"

"Hi, Mom and Dad. I'm okay."

"Okay, Sister, please tell us why we are here."

"I caught John cheating on his history test today."

"Is that true son?"

"Dad, I wasn't cheating. I don't cheat."

Then Sister jumped back into the conversation and told them the whole ordeal with Butch. Then Mom said, "Sister, Butch and John are good buddies and are always doing silly things. It sounds like Butch was just having a little fun. And besides that, Sister, if John said he wasn't cheating, he WASN'T CHEATING."

Before Sister could respond to Mom, I said, "Mom, he was just goofing around. Butch knows I don't cheat. Besides, I was just starting to take the test when it happened. I only answered one question."

Oh, my stomach hurt. I asked the teacher, "Can I go to the bathroom, Sister?"

"GO!"

I got there just in time! I was gone for 5-10 minutes. When I got back, Dad and Mom were standing.

Mom put her arm around me with a worried look and asked, "Are you okay John?"

"I'm okay."

Then Sister spoke. "John, I'm going to let you take the test over again. But you and George have got to stop this disruptive behavior."

"Okay, Sister. Thank you."

I'm not sure what happened while I was in the bathroom, but I think Mom and Dad love me.

You know, some days in your life you never, never forget ... and this was one of those days. It was a good day, though. It was fun; it was stressful. It was sprinkled with love; it was full of laughter. Got in trouble. Got a stomachache. But you know what?

GOT AN 'A-' ON MY HISTORY TEST!

Chapter 33

SNAKES IN SCHOOL

"And in the Boys' Room, Too"

Dateline: September 1955 – Ages 11 & 10

We were entertained by anything that walked, crawled, flew, swam, hopped or wiggled. One of our very favorites was snakes. There were hundreds and hundreds of garter snakes in our neighborhood, with the greatest concentration in Dr. Reese Anneberg's backyard. Dr. Anneberg lived one block west of us and, in his backyard, was a beautiful rock garden. In the rock garden, were many large, flat rocks and under those rocks lived snakes, snakes and more snakes.

We'd flip a couple of those rocks over and dozens of snakes would scurry in every direction. We'd grab the little ones and put them in our pockets and glass jars and the big ones we'd step on and then grab them by the back of the head. If we didn't do it just right with those big guys, they'd strike and bite us. That hurt like heck. Sometimes, they would even draw blood. That ended up being their last meal because we'd get mad and have to send them to snaky heaven.

It was the little buggers we enjoyed the most—the three to four inchers. They were fast and their bites didn't hurt. We would line them up and race them in the grass, the sidewalks, the streets, and sometimes even *in the house!*

Yes, we would take them in the house when Mom wasn't home and race them on the carpet on the living room floor. Boy, could they ever scoot on that carpet! One day when Mom was supposed to be gone, she caught us racing about six of those little guys on the living room carpet.

She got really, really mad at us and made us promise we would never, ever bring snakes into the living room again. We promised, and we never did bring them into the *living room* again.

We did, however, bring them up to the Boys' Room occasionally. Mom never caught us and we never did tell her, but we had some great races in our bedroom. One time, we lined up ten of those cute little snakes and turned them loose. They didn't go very straight. As a matter of fact, they went in every direction. We could only find five of them, so the other five just made a home somewhere in our bedroom. No big deal. We liked snakes, so we were good with it.

The snake thing really came to a head in September, 1955. Snap filled a sliding cigarette box with four of our three inch little friends and took them to school. After opening prayer, he got the attention of some of the girls and opened the box. The girls screamed! The boys cheered! And *Snake-Handler Snap* got kicked out of school.

When he got home, Mom was beside herself. She glared at the little guy and inquired, "What is the matter with you? You're nine years old and you just got kicked out of school!"

"Sorry, Mom."

"I don't care if you are sorry. Why in the world did you take snakes to school? I thought you promised to never bring snakes into the house."

"The school is not the house!"

"Yes, it is! A house is a school, a building, an office ... any place inside!"

"Sorry!"

"No, you're not. Now, why did you take those snakes into school?"

"To scare the girls."

"To scare the girls? Well, it worked. You scared the girls, the boys, the teachers and everyone else in the school! Snakes are scary and should never be let loose in any building, in any room, at any time! How would you like it if there were snakes crawling around in the Boys' Room?"

"There are."

"What did you say?"

"NOTHIN'!"

Chapter 34

RUMBLE

Dateline: 1960 Ages 15 & 16

This was the first summer I had my driver's license. One of the most exciting things to do at that time was "shag-the-drag!" That was simply driving back and forth on a stretch of Highway 30, from the old 71-30 Motel to what was then Farner-Bocken on the east side of town.

Back and forth we'd go for hours, honking at friends and other people, and hollering out the windows at friends and other people. We were never looking for trouble. We were just looking for fun.

There was, however, an older group of guys that shagged the drag on weekend nights that scared the crap out of us. They were the Night Hawks. They drove shiny old souped-up cars, wore black leather jackets or black tee-shirts (depending on the weather), and had long hair, smothered in greasy Brill

Cream, combed back into ducktails. They all smoked and had a reputation for being tough and mighty good with their fists.

In reality, the Night Hawks were pretty good guys. They all worked in the Carroll area and were law-abiding citizens. It's just that, at this time in history, the California "Hells Angels" were getting a lot of attention in the news, so we thought of the Night Hawks as Carroll's "Hells Angels." Actually, it was pretty cool to have a gang of our own in little old Carroll, Iowa.

We didn't mess with the Night Hawks when we were on the drag. If they pulled up beside us, we'd just look straight ahead or give them a polite hand salute. They wouldn't wave back. They would just give us a stern nod of the head and roll right on past us. I'll tell you what ... those guys were cool and scary at the same time. Deep down, we admired them. They helped make Carroll a colorful and exciting place in the 60s.

As you know, however, some teenagers do stupid stuff, and one night a bunch of us guys did something *really* stupid. We challenged a couple Night Hawks to a rumble.

Here's what happened.

It was a Friday night, and we had two car loads of guys, four in each car, shagging the drag and making a lot of noise. We sure weren't looking for the Night Hawks, but two of them pulled up alongside our lead car and just hung next to us. Normally, they'd pull away, but this night they didn't. They obviously wanted our attention. One of the guys in our car hollered something at them about "grease balls."

Now, how stupid was that?

The Night Hawks immediately responded with the middle finger salute. That got it started. We saluted them back. Then the words started flying, and before long, some idiot in the back seat said, "Let's rumble!"

We really didn't want to fight those guys, but if we had to, we liked the odds. There were eight of us and only two of them. Funny thing though, they didn't look a bit scared. The driver just said, "Okay. Where do you want it?"

"Southside Park!"

"Okay. We'll see you girls there in a few minutes."

So, it was on. Eight of us mouthy high school punks were about to take on two mighty Night Hawks. However, when we got to the Southside Park there was a major problem––a second Night Hawk car arrived with two more Night Hawks!

Did we stay and fight?

Heck no! We didn't like the odds. There were four of them and ...

ONLY EIGHT OF US!

Chapter 35

CORNFIELDS & GRAVEYARDS

"Car Trouble"

Dateline: 1959 to 1961 – Ages 15 to 17

All of our lives, Snap and I loved sports and played them every day. We also enjoyed the sport of hunting. When we were in high school at Kuemper Catholic in Carroll, Iowa, we played football, basketball and ran track.

Most days, when practice was over, we'd grab our shotguns and head for the country. Mom was always good about letting us use her car, a 1939 light blue Plymouth, three-on-the-floor with running boards and a throttle on the dash. We knew very little about cars, but we could drive them. The running boards and the throttle gave us a huge advantage when it came to hunting jackrabbits.

Thousands and thousands of those beautiful jackrabbits inhabited the farm fields of Carroll County, and they were fun and profitable to hunt. We would drive Mom's car out into picked cornfields, put the front tires in the narrow corn rows, pull the throttle out to approximately 10-15 miles an hour, open both front car doors, roll the windows down, step out onto the running boards, lean through the car door windows with our shotguns, and travel up and down those cornfields, harvesting dozens of jackrabbits.

We filled the trunk with our bounty and then drove to the Unckelman Mink Farm, which was a mile south of Carroll on Highway 71, and sold them for 75-cents each. Heck, gas was only about 25-cents a gallon back then, and a box of bullets was only a dollar, so we were money ahead!

We never did tell Mom and Dad that we drove that car in the cornfields, but it was pretty obvious to all who saw that old Plymouth moving along the streets of Carroll that those corn stalks sticking out from underneath had to have come from someone's field. One evening at the supper table, Mom made it painfully clear to us that we "better not ever, ever drive that car into another cornfield."

She was embarrassed to drive her car around town with cornstalks "hanging out everywhere." She said we couldn't use the car again unless we promised, "no more cornfields."

We promised.

A couple days later, on a Saturday, we piled into Mom's car and headed for the country. The hunt was on. We drove out to the farm where our friends, Larry and Dean Feld, lived. We picked those guys up and drove into one of their cornfields.

We weren't very honorable young men sometimes and this was one of those times. We really believed we could get away with it if we just removed the cornstalks after the hunt.

Good plan. Bad boys.

We were right in the middle of this big, long cornfield when the car started to cough and sputter and sputter some more and belch out big puffs of black smoke. We got scared and bailed out of that old war wagon, running as fast and as far as we could before it blew up!

Well, it didn't blow up. It coughed up a little more black smoke and then just lay there. It growled a bit, then it got real quiet. It was dead. Real dead!

And, so were we.

Thank God the Feld boys' farm wasn't far away, so we walked there and they gave us a ride home. When we walked in the front door, Mom was there to greet us and asked, "How was hunting, boys?"

I said, "Not so good, Mom."

Then she looked out the door and said, "Where's my car?"

Snap said, "We had a little problem."

She then demanded, "Boys, where is my car?"

"Mom, it ... ah ... broke. And, it's in a cornfield ..."

More of and the Best of Me & Snap

"A CORNFIELD!!! & $%^&*+#*@!!!!"

Somehow Mom and Dad found a way to forgive us, but it took about a month. Our family needed two vehicles, so Dad bought another car for Mom.

This one was a beauty––a 1953, two-tone brown, three-speed Plymouth with a radio that actually worked! They told us we could use it occasionally, but if we ever drove it in another cornfield we'd be grounded until we were fifty. We believed them, so this time we complied. That car never, ever went into a cornfield––ever. However, on occasion, it did go *into a cemetery.*

I don't recall who got the bright idea to do this, but once in awhile a bunch of us would go to the Carroll cemetery at night and play car tag. Yup, car tag (no one ever accused me and Snap and our buddies of being Rhodes Scholars)! The car that was "it" chased the other cars around the cemetery and when he caught one––rammed it––I mean, gently bumped the bumper––then that car was "it." We didn't do this very often, but the last time we did it we got in big, big trouble with the cops.

It was a cold winter night at about 11 o'clock, and six of us were playing car tag in the graveyard. We were having good, clean fun when a police cruiser pulled up to the cemetery entrance with red lights flashing. There was another exit, so we decided to run for it. We got about a hundred yards away from getting out of there when another cruiser with red lights flashing blocked our escape. Nowhere to go!

We were trapped. We were scared. And, we were in deep, deep trouble! We were ordered to, "Get out of your cars, and don't even *think* about running!"

Four cops converged on us with flashlights. They told us we were breaking the law and that we were "pretty stupid." We didn't know we were breaking the law, but we did know we were stupid.

Anyway, one of the cops there that night was a Top Cop. He was tough, so we feared and admired him at the same time. He did a lot to keep our town a safe place to live. No one ever did "give no lip" to this cop.

He took down our names, addresses, telephone numbers, and parents' names. Then he gave us a serious butt chewin' and told us to go home and wake up our parents and tell them what happened. He would personally be calling them in the morning. Then he said, "Now, get the hell out of this cemetery and don't ever, ever come back––unless you're dead!"

That one made us laugh a little bit. Then we thanked him and "got the hell out of there!"

When we got home, we went upstairs to Mom and Dad's bedroom and softly said, "Dad, can we talk to you?"

The light went on immediately and he said, "Is there a problem boys?"

"Kinda."

He told us to go down to the living room and he'd be there in a minute. When he got there, we told him everything. He didn't seem real mad, but seemed a little puzzled. So, to promote clarity, he conducted the following interrogation!

"So, you boys and some of your friends were driving around in the cemetery with your lights off, playing tag by banging into the other guy's car. Is that right?"

"Well, we really weren't banging that hard. We would just run into the other guy's bumper. And the guy that was "it" had to have his lights on. That was the rule."

"That was the rule?"

"Yes, sir."

"Did you know *your rules* had nothing to do with the fact that you were breaking the law?"

"Yes. I mean, we know it was stupid."

"Did you have beer in the car?"

"No, Dad. We don't drink."

"Did the police look for beer in your car?"

"Yes!"

"Did they find any?"

"Dad, we don't drink."

"So, they didn't find anything?"

"Well, they didn't find any beer, but they did find some cigars."

"Cigars? Do you boys smoke cigars?"

"Not really, Dad, but ... sometimes."

"Okay boys, up to bed, and don't tell your mother what happened. I'll tell her."

"Are we grounded?"

"Should you be?"

"YES!"

We went upstairs and Mom was there. She asked if we were okay, and we told her yes. We brushed our teeth, said a quick prayer by our bed, and climbed in. Mom came in and sprinkled Holy Water on us as she did every night, kissed our foreheads, and told us she loved us. We were eager to respond, "Love you too, Mom!"

As she left our room and was going into her bedroom, we heard this muffled exchange, "What did they do now, Bob?"

"Lorraine, you're not going to believe this one!"

"WANNA BET?"

Chapter 36

LONG-SHOTS

"Jail Time?"

Dateline: Fall, 1955 – Ages 11 & 10

Boys will be boys. And, even in the strict atmosphere of St. Lawrence Catholic Grade School, we did some idiotic things. One such thing was a game we played known as "Long-shots." This was a bathroom contest to see who could pee the farthest. The contestants would stand up as close as possible to the urinal, and then at someone's command, would take a single step back. Then another. Then another. And ... the longest shot wins. It wasn't very complicated and most of the guys we ran with did it quite frequently.

Anyway, one day during the noon hour, four of us lined up for "Long-shots." It was me, Snap, Tony and Tank. We were all pretty even when, on our third step back, one of the nuns hollered in, "What are you boys doing? Get out here right now!"

Crap, the last guy in forgot to shut the door; and as Sister was walking by, she got a good look at "Long-shots." We were in deep, deep trouble and pretty embarrassed, too.

Sister escorted us to the Principal's office and told us to tell the Principal, Sister Superior, what we were doing. Sister Superior looked right at me and said, "Well, John, let's start with you."

I fumbled and stumbled around, red-faced, and finally blurted it out, and then said, "Sorry, Sister."

The other guys did the same. Then, there was dead silence for what seemed like a long, long time. Finally, Sister asked me what our telephone number was and she called Mom.

When Mom answered, Sister said, "Mrs. Bruner, this is Sister Superior at St. Lawrence. I have John and Snap in my office."

"Oh, Sister, what did they do now?"

"Mrs. Bruner, they were caught doing long-shots in the bathroom."

"I'm so sorry, Sister. Those boys know they should only do long-shots outside on the playground."

"Oh no, Mrs. Bruner! If they did these kinds of long-shots outside on the playground ...

"THEY'D BE IN JAIL!"

Chapter 37

WHACK!

"I Think She Loves Us"

Dateline: October 1957, Ages 12 & 13

It was a rainy October day after school. Me and Snap were up in the Boys' Room changing out of our school clothes into our jeans and sweatshirts.

Well, we started bumping and pushing each other and, before long, we were in a full blown wrestling match. We weren't mad. We were just enjoying throwing the other guy on the floor, on the bed, into the wall, and any other place we could get a commanding hold. It was fun! We were really rockin' and rollin' when Mom hollered, "Boys, knock it off! It sounds like the ceiling is going to come down. Now, get your jeans on and get your fannies outside."

"But, it's raining outside!"

"I don't care. Take your rough-housing outside. NOW!"

Snap and I put on our tennis shoes and fully intended to go outside, but as so frequently happened, one guy bumped the other guy and away we went––wrestling from one end of the Boys' Room to the other.

It was fun, but stupid. And before we realized what we had done, there stood Mom looking down on us and holding something in her hand. We stopped wrestling, stood up and kinda smiled at Mom. She didn't smile back.

With that she asked, "Do you know what this is?"

"Part of the ceiling?"

"Yes. They call it ceiling tile and it's supposed to be on the ceiling––not in my hand. So, why isn't it on the ceiling?"

"Sorry, Mom. We probably knocked it down when we were wrestling."

"You aren't sorry now, but you are going to be sorry in just a minute."

With that she threw the ceiling tile on Snap's bed, left the room and returned twenty seconds later with one of Dad's belts.

"I'm sick and tired of you boys not minding me! Now, bend over and grab your ankles."

"Mom, what's with the belt? What's wrong with spankings?"

"You're too old and too big and spankings never worked anyway. Now bend over!"

Wouldn't you know? Snap had a plan. He said, "Okay, we will, but before we do, we have a confession to make—we broke the light above Toad's bed."

When Mom turned her head to look, Snap grabbed the belt right out of her hand. She looked shocked and mad and said, "Give me that belt!"

Snap fired back, "If I do, will you promise not to whack us really hard?"

Mom was really getting irritated, "Give me that belt!"

Snap persisted, "Not until you promise."

"Okay, I've had it! I'm calling your father."

We both responded simultaneously, "NO! NO! NO! Don't call Dad!"

With that, Snap put the belt back in Mom's hand and pleaded, "Please, Mom, don't call Dad. Please?! Look, we're ready."

And with that we stood there side-by-side and bent over and grabbed our ankles.

That worked. She grabbed the belt and said, "Now, let's get this over with."

But, before she could deliver the first blow, I said, "Mom, please don't whack us too hard. We are big boys now and we don't want you to see us cry."

Snap added, "Yeah, Mom, but if you do whack us hard, we want you to know that ... we still love you."

That broke her! We could now hear serious laughter in her voice as she said, "Dear God, what am I going to do with these two?"

Snap answered with, "Pray for us?"

Mom responded, "That doesn't work either!"

Then she totally lost it. She couldn't stop laughing. After trying to regain her composure for a minute or so, she walked towards the door, dropped Dad's belt on brother Toad's bed, exited the room and with one last reminder that we were still in trouble––BANG!

She slammed the door.

We straightened up, smiled triumphantly at each other and then Snap said ...

"JOHN, I THINK SHE LOVES US!"

Chapter 38

KISSIN' IN THE CHICKEN COOP

"A Magical Moment"

Dateline: Fall, 1960 – Ages 16 & 15

It was a beautiful fall, Friday night. The high school football season was over, so we were free to do whatever we wanted and decided to double date. Snap wasn't old enough for his license yet, so I had the privilege of driving us around in our Mom's 1939, beautiful, light blue Plymouth. You know, that old car had corn stalks sticking out from under it—but that's another story.

Anyway, Snap's girlfriend lived in town and my girlfriend, Connie Schreck, was a country girl who lived seven miles out of town. I asked Snap if he and his date would like to ride with me to pick up Connie and he said, "No, her folks are out for the evening, so I will just stay at her house and when you guys get back to town, pick us up. But don't get in a big hurry."

"Don't get in hurry? Oh, I get it!"

I was driving as fast as that old car could go. I couldn't wait to see Connie. She was so special. I hadn't ever met anyone like her before. We had only been dating a month and she was a senior and I was a junior, but that didn't seem to matter. We just enjoyed hanging out together.

When I arrived, we sat around the living room with her folks and just visited. What wonderful people they were. They made me feel right at home and I loved that. After about a half hour the conversation somehow turned to the brooder house that was currently full of baby chicks––dozens of them! Since I had shared my pigeon stories with them, Connie's mom, Rose, suggested that Connie take me to the brooder house to see all these little creatures. It was a great idea. I was excited to go there and also happy to spend some time alone with Connie.

We entered the brooder house (I always called it the chicken coop). There they were: dozens of cute, tiny, cuddly, baby chicks. Connie invited me to pull up a seat so we both grabbed a five gallon feed bucket, turned it upside-down and settled in for a very special event.

As the chicks swarmed around us, Connie picked one of them up and said, "John, watch this."

She laid the little chick on its back in the palm of her hand and ever so gently rubbed on its tiny little neck and breast. After 10 -15 seconds of this, the little guy rested his head back, closed his eyes, unfolded his wings and went into a deep slumber. Darndest thing I had ever seen. Then I tried it, and to my great surprise, it worked. She did it again and so did I. Within ten minutes, half the chicks in that chicken coop were asleep at our feet. The little chicks would wake up and run back to us and we were just laughing and laughing; loving every moment of it and our time together.

As we picked up the chicks, our hands would occasionally touch and we'd look at each other and smile. Something magical was happening. I turned, and looking into her beautiful, beautiful face and with all the courage I could muster out of my skinny 135-pound body, I asked, almost in a whisper, "Can I kiss you?"

Her eyes gave a brief flutter and she said, "Okay."

At that moment we very cautiously ... very tenderly ... very lovingly ... kissed ... in the chicken coop. That was November, 1960.

On September 4, 1965 ...

WE WERE MARRIED!

Chapter 39

SNAP'S ON FIRE

"Farts with Flames"

Dateline: Christmas Eve, 1958 – Ages 14 & 13

When we were growing up, our fun time and play time repertoire was full of wrestling, boxing, fishing, basketball, football, telling the truth, telling lies, climbing trees, falling out of trees, playing on roof tops, falling off roof tops, riding horses, getting bucked off horses, camping, trapping, making kites, flying kites, cops and robbers, strip poker, pool, tents, cigars, forts, and ... *farts*!

Okay, we weren't vulgar little boys; we were just normal little guys. We learned stuff. We tried stuff. One day we added "lighting farts" to our list of daily activities.

Our good buddy Cy Farner told us about it.

We told him we didn't believe it, so he got down on his back on his kitchen floor (no one was home), waited a few minutes, struck a match, held it down by the seat of his pants, and ...

BANG!

Lighting shot out of his butt.

COOL!! It was easy, harmless, and it was fun!

We learned this when we were about eight or nine and engaged in this activity with great regularity. We were couth little guys and always did this privately, very seldom bragging about the exceptionally "good ones."

However, there was one that topped them all. It was Christmas Eve, 1958. Mom served her traditional, wonderful oyster stew, chili, pies and candy––you name it, Mom had it there for us. There was no better mom, or cook, in the whole world, and we ate it all. We opened presents, laughed, talked and teased until about 11:00, then Dad announced it was time for bed. Santa was on his way and we were going to 8:00 Mass in the morning. While we were helping pick up, Snap accidentally passed gas. Oh, it was ripe––really ripe––and I dared him to light "one of those things." Our younger brother, Barry, who was six at the time, told us to quit talking dirty. I told him, "Farts are natural gas and you really can light them!"

He said, "Liar."

We told him to stick around and watch.

Dad, Mom (who was pregnant with brother Dave), and sisters, Judy and Mary Fran, headed upstairs to bed. Snap and

I told them we wanted to show Toad something and we'd be right up. (Toad was little brother Barry's nickname.)

Our Uncle Stan and Aunt Gertrude gave us the same present every Christmas––fuzzy cotton pajamas, which we were wearing. We were in the living room. I turned the lights off, Snap laid down on his back (remember we only did this with pants on), struck a match, expelled one of those nasty things, and:

"KABOOM!"

I've never seen such bright, brilliant colors in my whole life! And, it's the first and last time I have ever seen a human being totally engulfed in flames. The combination of fuzzy pajamas and that gas explosion had old Snap torched from top to toes.

Barry screamed and ran upstairs. Snap sprang to his feet and I was whacking him with a throw rug. The burn time was probably five to six seconds. He wasn't hurt a bit, but those pajamas sure looked and smelled awful! Snap about burned up on that Christmas Eve, but we couldn't stop laughing.

As a matter of fact, that was fifty years ago...

AND WE ARE STILL LAUGHING!

Chapter 40

BEER

"Yes?"

Dateline:?

It was a hot, sultry August afternoon. Me and Snap were in the Boys' Room just shootin' the bull about all the stuff we did and all the times we got caught and all the times we *didn't* get caught. It was a good talk, until it turned to, "Who can take who?"

We started bumping each other and were just about to get into another full-blown wrestling match when Mom came in.

"Boys, what are you doing?"

"Nothin'!"

"Don't give me that. You were about to start wrestling again, weren't you?"

"Guess so."

"When are you boys going to learn? You are both getting too big and too old for this stuff."

"You're right, Mom."

"You're darn right, I'm right! And if you two don't stop this, one or both of you are going to get hurt and I'm getting sick and tired of going up to that hospital. *I've been up there so much with you two, people think I work there!"*

"Good one, Mom!"

"Listen boys, I've got something I need to do. So, please promise me you WON'T wrestle!"

"Okay, we promise. We won't wrestle."

"Thank you. Now, go outside and find something to do."

Mom was serious and so were we––no more wrestling. We visited a little bit longer, then decided to head for the Jungle.

As we got downstairs, we realized there wasn't anybody around. They were all gone. We went into the kitchen and I opened the fridge. We were both really thirsty. There was milk, water, and juice, but no pop, no Kool-Aid, and no lemonade. But, on the bottom shelf, was beer––COLD BEER!

I said, "Snap, let's have a beer."

"Are you serious?"

"Sure, I am! Here."

I handed him a beer and took one for myself. We slipped out the family room door and into the backyard. We had no sooner opened our beer and taken a drink, than who appears out of nowhere? *MOM!* She had been out tending to her flowers.

She came up to me, grabbed my beer, put it up to her mouth and took a big drink. Our dear mother, Lovey, followed this astonishing act by snatching Snap's beer and doing the same thing to his. She then took a deep breath and handed our beers back to us. We were SHOCKED!

Looking at both of us, straight in the eyes, Mom said, "I don't usually like beer, but on hot days like this it sure tastes good."

Wait a minute! Is something not right here? Is Mom condoning juvenile beer drinking? *No, not at all!* The misunderstanding is my fault. You see, at the beginning of this chapter, I didn't record the dateline. But now it's time for you to know. It was 1999. Mom was 80 years old and Dad was 85!

Me and Snap? Well, I was 55 and Snap was 54. So you see, we were plenty old enough to legally drink beer!

But, this story is not over! Mom said, "Remember a little while ago when we were up in the Boys' Room and I asked you not to wrestle? Do you remember that?"

"Yes, Mom."

"Well, did you obey me or did you go ahead and wrestle anyway?"

"Come on, Mom. You know the answer to that."

"Well, did you or didn't you wrestle up in the Boys' Room?"

"Heck, NO! Do you think at our age we're that stupid?"

"YES!"

Printed in the United States
By Bookmasters